John Hannon

ENGAGED

MANAGEMENT
VOLUME 2

Arrives August, 2016

Order your $19.95 copy today:
robin@jimdoyle.com
941-926-7355

ENGAGED MANAGEMENT

VOLUME 1
INSPIRING YOUR TEAM TO WIN

JOHN HANNON

ENGAGED MANAGEMENT
VOLUME 1
INSPIRING YOUR TEAM TO WIN

Jim Doyle & Associates
7711 Holiday Drive
Sarasota, FL 34231

(941) 926-7355
FAX: (941) 925-1114
John@jimdoyle.com
www.jimdoyle.com
www.doyleondemand.com

Copyright First Edition ©2016
John M. Hannon
Jim Doyle & Associates, Inc.
Edited by Robin Renna
Cover design by Bydand Creative
Cover Photo by Booth Photography

To my wife Bridget, daughters Madison and Cara, and son Evan. The words on these pages and pursuit of my passion are only possible because of your unwavering support, patience, and love.

CONTENTS

Chapter 3
<u>Managing For Maximum Performance</u>

CHAPTER 4
SALES PREPARATION AND PLANNING

CHAPTER 5
WITHOUT CUSTOMERS YOU HAVE NO BUSINESS

CHAPTER 6
FOCUS ON YOUR CAREER

ACKNOWLEDGEMENTS

Deep appreciation marks only the beginning of my feelings for the many individuals who helped inspire and push me to take action to move my thoughts from concept to book.

Lucky for me, Robin Renna is our Director of Client Relations at Jim Doyle & Associates (JDA). She authored an award-winning children's book called *Kumba's Courage* and has served as the editor for multiple business books. Naturally, she was an easy pick to edit this project. She gets a giant thank you trophy for professional patience as I repeatedly missed deadlines, making her interactions with vendors, clients, and illustrators more cumbersome than it should have been.

Most in the television business recognize Jim Doyle as the industry's leading keynote speaker, teacher/trainer, and author. It's amazing to witness his interaction with audiences and his ability to move them to action. But what the crowd may not know about Jim is his heart of service, his value of generosity, and his never-ending passion for giving. He is the definitive example of human connection. I am so grateful for the opportunity to lead the company that bears his name, and proud to refer to Jim as a mentor, business partner, and friend.

Unfortunately, because of our travel schedules, Tom Ray, Pat Norris, and I are only in the office together a couple of times a month. I'm so thankful to be in the company of Tom and Pat, two incredible marketing minds with contagious enthusiasm for our industry.

Many of the articles in these pages have resulted from random catch-up conversations, not only with Tom and Pat, but with the entire JDA "world headquarters" team of Elaine, Matt, Lynne, Anne, and Sue. If there is such a thing as a well-oiled office environment, this is it. To an individual, each possesses a want of service, making your priority our priority. I am humbled to work so closely with such stars.

Our Senior Marketing Consultants (SMC)—our road warriors—spend up to 28 weeks a year traveling, reinforcing our UPGRADE Selling® process, and generating revenue for our partner stations. To maintain a schedule like that takes incredible personal and family sacrifice. The SMCs often deserve more thanks than they receive and I am forever indebted for their commitment to the success of our customers.

To maximize our ability to help our client partners, it is important for our company to be ahead of the rapid changes in the television industry. I ask a lot of questions and learn something new in nearly every client conversation. Many of those learned lessons are in this book. Thank you, our client partners, customers and friends, for the trust and confidence you place in us. We absolutely value your loyalty and are keenly aware that without your support we have no business.

In 2010, Billy Bruce (my friend since 3rd grade) and I, attended a "how to write a book" workshop. Bill is an accomplished writer who has a reputation for penning positive community impact stories for local newspapers and magazines. When the topic of me writing a book was tabled, he was the first to ask, "Why not?" Thank you, Bill, for being a lifelong friend and for always being a shining beacon of "you can do it."

Sometimes, I can be philosophical in thought recalling the many men and women who have had such a positive impact on shaping my career *and* life. At the risk of sounding like an Emmy winner forgetting to thank a Hollywood big wig, my gratitude list is entirely too long to detail here. You know who you are. If at this moment, you find yourself wondering if I am speaking of you, indeed I am.

Collectively, the many interactions with these mentors, teachers, managers, leaders, co-workers, family, neighbors, and friends has seeded an overwhelming desire to deliver to others the lifetime gifts that have been so generously provided to me.

John Hannon
Sarasota, Florida
March 2016

FOREWORD

I read a lot of books on management and leadership. Have you noticed that most of the people who write those books don't run companies? They're consultants. They write about leadership but they don't practice it. That's part of what makes this book different. This is a book about becoming a better manager from someone who is not only great at managing but is also a great leader.

I ought to know. I selected John Hannon to lead my company, and it's been just about the best decision I've ever made.

If you ask any entrepreneur, they'll tell you that their business is like their baby. If you can connect with how, after 25 years, Jim Doyle & Associates is like my baby, you might be able to understand how much I respect John Hannon. I made him the President of my baby a year or so ago after he had worked with us for 3 years, and it's been a great decision.

I was able to see John's passion and enthusiasm for the TV business long before I ever reached out to talk to him about joining our company. He had built an industry reputation as a great manager and leader during his career stops at ABC, FOX, and NBC affiliated stations. Then he took the stand-alone CW station in Dayton, Ohio, and made it the standard for CW's around the country—both as a ratings and a revenue success. That led to a corporate job with Acme Communications and similar success as he took his style of management and leadership to their stations and national morning news distribution. When Acme was sold, I made a phone call to John. It was one of the best phone calls I have ever made.

I have watched, up close, how engaged John is with our staff and with every facet of our company, and I think I have a pretty clear sense of what that means. It means articulating a strategy to grow the business and position it for the future. It means clear expectations, and with that the opportunity for real accountability. It's about making sure the people that you lead know where they stand and where the company is headed. He doesn't just get people to follow him, he creates a culture in which they're excited to be participants in reaching and exceeding company goals.

John's brand of engaged management has certainly made a difference for Jim Doyle & Associates. We are setting revenue and profit records year after year. John has solved a long-term problem we had of being slow to market with new products, but even more importantly, we are delivering the best results ever for our clients because John has implemented the ideas that are outlined in this book. These ideas can make a huge difference in your business as well.

John is more than a great leader. He's a great Dad, husband, and friend. He's changed our company in so many positive ways, while always being respectful to a founder with strong opinions. He's the real deal. Trust me. I have seen that up close and personal.

I like books that are real world. Books that outline practical solutions. Books that motivate me to be better, while at the same time reconnecting me with things I already knew but might have drifted away from. *Engaged Management* is that kind of book. I know it will help you to inspire your team in a more effective way.

The TV business you and I love is undergoing fundamental changes. A new world requires us to become better. Staying the same is a prescription for disaster. We can't stay the same! So use this book as a roadmap for your personal and professional growth. It will make you better!

Jim Doyle

INTRODUCTION

We live in an attention-starved world. It seems there's never enough time to do the things we need or want to do. We have become a society of headline consumers, where communicating in 6 second videos and 140 characters is not only preferred, but acceptable.

With those thoughts in mind, this first of a multi-volume book series you're holding today *is not* a business book where each chapter is an organized step to becoming a better manager. Instead, it's a compilation of self-contained articles featuring anecdotes, stories, and voice of experience observations. The concept for this project originated from my weekly writings for members of *The Leaders Edge*, our TV broadcasting and cable management coaching program.

"Your bosses can give you a management title, but only your team members or employees can designate you a leader."

In selecting the title *Engaged Management*, I wanted to stay true to the title your bosses have given or one day will give to you. But it's important to be clear that while a title does make you a manager on an office organizational chart, your actions and example will make you a leader, and ultimately, the most successful managers are leaders. They establish and get buy-in to a vision, hold team members accountable, and praise superior achievement. A leader has the ability to consistently generate positive momentum by being available and in the moment. Simply put, with an eye to constructing a culture of team success, managers who lead are "engaged" with individuals, developing a unique understanding of the "inspiration" each needs in order to "win."

CHAPTER 1

LEADING THE TEAM

Become the kind of leader that people would follow voluntarily; even if you had no title or position. -Brian Tracy

THE LEADER ADJUSTS THE SAILS

Did you see the headline about the broadcasting company buying another broadcasting company? Fill in the blanks with a surprise or not-so-surprise announcement of your own. As of this writing, there is no denying that our industry is in the middle of a buy and sell frenzy. As *TVNewsCheck* editor and co-publisher Harry Jessell wrote, "The 'M&A Thunder' Just Keeps Rolling," "...everything appears to be in play." There have even been reports of merger discussions involving names like Cablevision, Charter, and Time Warner, proving that cable is not sitting idly by as broadcasters continue to consolidate.

Just as you're looking for answers, most certainly your AE's are seeing their employer's name in the trades and coming to you looking for answers. So, what do you tell them? The best advice is to encourage them to do their absolute best work. There is no better moment to shine than when a company is in transition. The most valuable assets to any company are competent and high-performing personnel. If your sellers are identified as such, whether the company is being bought or sold, they will likely prosper through the change.

What about managers? To you, I would say the same thing. Now is the moment for your absolute best work. There was a time when the acquiring company held all the cards and populated their new acquisitions with their own talent. However, today's companies are getting so big that they don't have enough of their own managers to transition to the new properties. This situation creates opportunity for managers of the acquired outlets.

It's an exciting time for our business, but it will be quite a while before the dust settles. Until then, consider this quote from John Maxwell, *"The pessimist complains about the wind. The optimist expects it to change. The leader adjusts the sails."*

GET YOUR TEAM MOVING IN THE RIGHT DIRECTION

Throughout the course of Olympic and political

windfall revenue years, there are big celebratory smiles. But behind closed doors, during quiet planning conversation, I will often encounter an equal number of frowns in anticipation of a difficult sales environment the upcoming year. Being curious, I always like to ask this question of media managers: "What are you going to do to prepare your team for sales success next year?"

The great managers are almost always already taking action.

Often times, the leadership of an organization is the single factor that determines success. Teams yearn for a strong leader—someone who can concisely and clearly communicate a vision and the steps needed to achieve a shared reward. Congratulations if you've already started preparing your sales pros. For those who haven't, the below steps will help you boost sales performance and get your team moving in the right direction:

- **Define Expectations**. This should not be a gray area. Talk in terms of percentage increases and categories like new business and local direct. All expectations should be defined by a timeline.
- **Set The Bar High But Be Realistic**. Push your sales pros to deliver new revenue highs, but take care to make sure the goals are realistic. Perceived "impossible" numbers can de-motivate sellers.

- **Play To Each Individual's Strength**. If an AE is having success selling a particular station initiative or category, consider offering them a "carrot" for additional exceptional sales to take full advantage of their positive momentum.
- **Provide Progress Checks—Often**. That which gets measured gets sold. Make sure to measure performance in the key priorities for your operation. Hold the AE accountable so resulting sales, or lack of, are not a surprise.
- **Levy Punishment For Poor Performance**. Don't be afraid to have a conversation with someone who's not pulling his or her weight. As a leader you owe it to the sales team to quickly address lack of performance. In extreme circumstances, pulling an account is necessary to provide a wake-up call to the underperformer.
- **Reward And Celebrate Success**. Better performance results in higher commissions. But for many account executives, money is not the only motivator. Make sure to recognize and reward extra effort that results in increased sales. Doing so creates a culture of high morale and continues to build sales confidence.

AE'S WANT A LEADER, NOT A MANAGER

"How to get to the decision maker" is one of our most often requested "asks" for help. I love teaching this session, as heads nod and light bulbs pop when sellers begin to realize that getting to the person who can say "yes" when everyone else says "no" is not an impossibility.

In one portion of the training, I explain that no matter what you do, some prospects are caught up in titles. If your title is not equal to or larger than the prospect's title, they will likely, at the beginning of a relationship, be slow to respond or, worse yet, not even return your call. My suggested solution is for AE's to go to their sales manager or general manager and ask for their help in placing a General-to-General call.

At the conclusion of this session, more often than I care to admit, a sheepish AE will approach me and ask if they can speak confidentially. The question goes something like this, "Uh, John, you said we should go to our sales manager or GM for help in calling a prospect hung up on job titles. Can you tell me, what should I do if my managers won't call a prospect or go on calls with me?"

My intent here is not to list the myriad of responses I run through with AE's when hit with this question. Instead, I want to discuss the root of the issue: managers who have time to manage but do not have time to lead.

It is commonly known that the demands upon television sales managers have escalated over the past few years. There are more stations, channels, products, personnel, regulations, and corporate minutia than ever before, despite the same 24 hours in a day. Managers can be very effective and even successful at navigating today's demands. However, just because one can "manage" does not necessarily mean he or she can "lead."

Ultimately, everyone on your sales team wants you to *lead* them, not *manage* them. Sellers want someone who can show vs. tell. They don't want a talking head to download do's and don'ts, only to stand at the entrance to the office at the end of the day wanting a full report on all sales presentations. Sales pros want to see you aren't afraid to get in the trenches, instead of hiding behind a closed door with report deadline excuses. They need to see you active, engaged, energetic, and first in line when it comes to helping them produce new revenue highs.

Somewhere along the line, sales management commitments got a bit reversed. Maybe we can point to consolidation for creating fear of loss or job insecurity. Whatever the root, many of today's television managers seem eager to satisfy corporate requests. Reporting and justification take precedent over dedicating time for the needs of the sales team.

From where I sit, that's backward thinking. Revenue solves all issues. If a manager would dedicate his/her time to being on the street with AE's, meeting clients, closing business, and in general being the example, then sales momentum, and ultimately revenue, would surely pick up. An often used phrase is *"lead by example."* Notice the word is "lead," not "manage." Which are you committed to being: a leader or a manager?

EMAIL IS NOT APPROPRIATE FOR EVERY MESSAGE

In training sessions, you may have heard me discourage your sellers from utilizing email to get appointments with sales prospects. This method of prospecting to meet clients allows reps, especially those with call reluctance, to hide behind email while getting you, the sales manager, off their back by confidently stating, "Yes, I contacted the client but they haven't responded."

Jim Doyle & Associates Senior Vice President, Pat Norris, tells a story of helping an auto dealer who complained of an extremely slow computer. During the computer's cleaning and defragging, Pat discovered the dealer had 9,974 *unopened* emails! How many requests for meetings from media reps do you think were in that mess of emails?

Let's switch gears for a second. As a manager and leader within your media outlet, what is your primary means of communication with your team? Is it email? Are there any topics you would not address via email? Is it possible that sometimes when faced with delivering uncomfortable feedback to team members we, as managers, hide behind our

9

email statements? From my experience, email is not appropriate for every message.

My good friend, Marty Grunder, is an accomplished author, speaker, and extremely successful entrepreneur and owner of Grunder Landscaping in Dayton, Ohio.

In an article from his Great Ideas weekly, he digs a bit deeper into this topic. After reading Marty's words below, I'm certain you'll think twice before you hit the send button the next time. (www.martygrunder.com)

So You Want To Be A Thought Leader, Eh?

In the past couple of weeks I've seen a few things from so-called "thought leaders" that make me say, "What?" One fella I follow on Twitter, whom I really admire for a certain business philosophy he teaches, had this to say about disciplining team members. (I don't use the word employees; long-time followers know that about me and so does my team.)

When an employee starts with your company or during their periodic reviews or when discussing ways to motivate your team, ask your employee how they want you to address disciplinary issues should they ever come up. Let them lay down the rules.

Do they want you to email them or write them a formal letter? Do they prefer you call them into your office for a private meeting? Do they prefer you take them offsite to a Starbucks for a heart-to-heart?

Document their preferred method in your HR file.

Okay, I sort of get where he's coming from, but under no circumstances is emailing discipline to a team member a way to go. Sure, if one of your folks forgot to lock a window or turn off the lights, maybe you email them. But if you have someone who said something inappropriate, made a mistake on a job that cost you a client, or countless other things, there's no way you email that. I agree with the blogger's comments about finding out how you "get through" to a team member, but in reading his post, I think I've exposed him, to a degree. There's no way he has managed a large team of people and, therefore, shouldn't be commenting on this type of issue. To be blunt, he's a thought leader on business, but not HR. I can't imagine there is an HR Guru who would agree with his post. And here's my point this week:

A thought leader is someone who has experience in a particular area. And it's not just the experience that's important, it's the learning that goes on from the experience. When email was first invented, I sent all sorts of emails with discipline in them and you know what I found out from that experience? It doesn't work! Emails are read wrong—the tonality is lost and people either read too much or not enough into them—but they rarely get it "just right," as Goldilocks would say.

My guess is that the thousand or so folks who

get my weekly great idea have the potential to be a "thought leader" on a topic. We are all experts on something. But none of us is an expert on everything, and experience is the real teacher. In fact, in my world of coaching, consulting, blogging, and the like, I try to stay focused on teaching things that I have experience with. So, you're never going to hear anything from me on accounting, using a transit, flying a plane, coaching football, physics, geology, sociology, or anything with "ology" in it. I'll stick to what I've tried, as experience is the best teacher of all.

And, in case you didn't get one of the many messages and rants in this week's Great Idea, don't email your team discipline. Instead, sit down with them and be inquisitive, not accusatory, and have a conversation. We're adults trying to run landscaping companies. You don't have all the answers nor do I. But together, we just might.

THE FOUR COMPONENTS OF A SUCCESSFUL OPERATION

If we've met, you have likely heard me tell and (re)tell, with great pride and enthusiasm, the story of my long ago experience as the General Manager of a very special team at a *stand-alone*

CW affiliate in Dayton, Ohio, owned then by ACME Communications. The station was in the national spotlight as the network's model affiliate and was the highest rated CW station for *four* consecutive years. The biggest source of pride was sales performance. Our baker's dozen sales department consistently left no stones unturned and delivered market revenue shares as high as #2 (national) and #3 (local). To quote our then national sales manager Billie Sue Adkins, "We captured lightning in a bottle."

The end of the story? Unfortunately, as is the tendency in the media business, the station was sold into a larger company duopoly and has since never achieved the same prominence.

Deep relationships and friendships develop out of rare, shared career experiences. As a result, most team members from the Dayton station have stayed in contact, despite having moved on to other opportunities. When two or more of the old gang get together, the conversation inevitably turns to, "Wow, remember when?"

That was the occasion over dinner with Al Yarcho, a former Dayton's CW difference-maker, vacationing in Tampa. After a bit of personal catch-up, our conversation quickly turned to the good old days. I asked Al, "Why was the station so successful? What was different compared to other media outlets?" When that question is posed to me, I often respond with explanations of seamless programming, promotional strategies, and sales call count percentages.

Al had an entirely different picture of why the operation was so successful. He boiled it down into *four* categories:

1. **Egos were checked at the door**
2. **Everyone listened and shared**
3. **The whole team participated in the good and the bad**
4. **"That's not my job" was not in the culture**

1. Egos Were Checked At The Door

In short of *ten* years, *seventeen* members of the Dayton team were promoted up, either within the station, the group, to a larger market, or to the network. Each department had a one or two person deep management bench who were being informally groomed and ready to step up. In that kind of environment, egos are usually kept in check as the talent gap between manager and team member is minimized, resulting in a mutual respect. The "team" was always greater than any "one" individual.

2. Everyone Listened And Shared

Input, from every level, was not only encouraged but expected. Brainstorms and planning sessions took place departmentally, station-wide, in teams for special tasks, and even with clients.

Some of our best sales training came from AE's with varied backgrounds. Sales promotion suggestions resulted in national awards. Practices like motivational quotes on agendas, guest speaker sessions, state-of-the-station breakfasts, and traveling quarterly parties grew from team input. Even the wall paint colors were selected by employee vote.

3. The Whole Team Participated In The Good And The Bad

Because every team member had "skin in the game," all shared in wins and losses. During sales contests, employees were assigned to an AE to cheerlead and motivate. As the AE racked up sales and points, the cheerleader also shared in the prize and/or cash rewards. At event and award dinners, instead of having one station representative, everyone who was responsible for the creation and submission was encouraged to attend and stand on the stage to bask in the victory.

However, when revenue or ratings slipped or project deadlines loomed, everyone on the team was equally willing to put in the hours and effort required to right the ship.

4. "That's Not My Job" Was Not In The Culture

We can all think of a GM who would encounter

a piece of trash in the hallway and direct someone else to pick it up instead of picking it up themselves. As leaders, we should be ever mindful that our employees are watching our every move. Over time, the team will model behavior.

One of the absolute best television industry managers, and an even better leader, Stan Gill, taught me that lesson. Stan and I still remain close and I consider him to be a great friend and one of my most influential mentors. He is responsible for laying the first "brick" in building the foundation and team that made the successful operation in Dayton possible. He was the definition of management by walking around. He was always visible, with endless energy, while observing, questioning, and challenging each team member to push beyond their self-defined limits.

Stan possessed a lot of pride for our facility. He would stop mid-sentence and bend over to pick up a stray paper wrapper in the hallway or straighten chairs on the way out of a meeting or jump in to help move tables after a party or load and unload them into a truck at events. His example sent the message that if the Vice President and General Manager can do this, no individual or title is exempt from helping improve our environment and culture.

Many years after Stan left the station, one could still see AE's clearing snow off team member cars, production staffers mopping floors, and department heads stacking chairs after luncheons. These unasked work "extras" were merely a reflection of the pride of team each employee possessed.

DO IT NOW

As a television sales manager, the concept of "Do It Now" is likely not foreign to you. However, I suspect that some of us may try to apply the theme to everything that crosses our desk, ends up in our email or is left on our voicemail. The key to "Do It Now" is to prioritize the most important things—the things that will have the most impact upon your goal—and to tackle those first.

In Brian Tracy's book, *Eat That Frog,* he suggests that the most impactful items should be at the top of your list to accomplish as soon as you start your day. Often, when adopting this strategy, managers find that the smaller, non-essential tasks fall off the list and are ultimately found to have absolutely no impact on achieving their most important goals. As of this writing, I have *three* suggestions for *top* priorities that should be on your "Do It Now" revenue goal list:

1) Health Care. Make sure your team is organized and ready to take advantage of the revenue opportunities resulting from new health care provisions. Thanks to the Affordable Care Act, exchanges have money, but that total pales in comparison to the dollars from insurance companies, hospitals and medical groups, and local doctors. Over the next few years, America's medical community will welcome up to 30 million previously uninsured patients. Competition to cater to these newly insured will be fierce. As with any category, the top of mind rep gets the money, but be patient (no pun intended) because healthcare uncertainty may delay some advertising agreements.

2) Auto. Your AE's need to get face to face with their auto dealers. This category is still a huge percentage of our industry's overall billing. Market analysts predict continued bounce-back and record unit sales thanks to pent-up demand, lower gas prices, easier financing, and low interest rates. Car dealers are happy and they need the power of your medium and digital products.

3) Digital. Have a formal plan for educating, training, and holding accountable on digital sales. Across the country business owners are begging for someone, *anyone*, to show them how to make sense out of all the available digital options. Make sure your reps understand the value of your digital plays because if they lack faith in the products, they will not sell them. Stop the local agencies from stealing *your* money by touting their agency's "digital expert." Make your AE's the most educated digital reps in the market and watch your cash register light up. A word of caution: practice and role-play speaking on the client's level. Often, when armed with new information, reps inadvertently speak over the client's head.

MAKE SURE GOALS CONNECT AT MULTIPLE LEVELS

We spend a lot of time in this business strategically planning and laying out accountability measures and road maps to achieve our business goals. But does it ever feel as though a goal was doomed before the first show of effort? No doubt, you are now recalling a time when a revenue budget was so high that it had a reverse performance effect on the staff. The consensus was something like, "There's no use in wearing ourselves out when we know we'll never come close to that number." That's not the direction I want to head in this writing.

In goal planning, the most important thing to understand is how each individual goal builds and fits into the big picture. The individual goals should feed your sales department goals, the sales department goals should support your station / media outlet or office goals, and lastly, the station or office goals should fulfill the corporate or group goals.

This diagram shows that it's a very simple triangle, which sometimes gets forgotten:

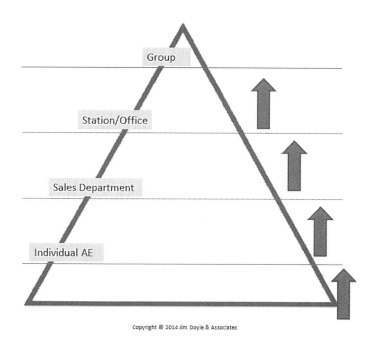

Take a minute to think about your family and personal goals. If your daughter has a goal of going to an expensive private college but you're saving for a community college education, at some point there's going to be a disconnect because the goals don't match.

The same is true in your work life. For example, if a large percentage increase in local direct revenue is a priority in your office, and a few AE's are spending the majority of their training time sharpening their agency negotiation skills, there's a disconnect. Their priority should be call volume on local, non-agency accounts. Each individual effort reinforces the local direct revenue goals of the department.

I'm reminded of the general sales manager who expressed frustration in his team's new business effort. The team barely peaked above 8% in new business to total billing. Their goal was 10% and the corporate expectation was 12%. Excuse me?

I had to ask, "Why do the team and corporate new business goals not match?" The GSM's response was something I'm confident he would never tell his corporate VP of Sales. "As a team, we have historically finished between 6% and 8% in new business billing. I thought the corporate mandate of 12% was a stretch for our folks, so I dropped the number to 10%, a number that was an improvement and a good showing."

Besides the outright disregard of corporate's wishes, do you see the problem with this GSM's logic? Let's say his team hits the ten percent new business goal. They will celebrate their effort and may even have a bonus expectation. However, in the eyes of the corporate managers, the ten percent performance is two points short of expectation. There will be no team congratulations or bonus. In fact, there will likely be the opposite—calls for justification of the shortfall.

The individual and department goals did not match and feed the station and corporate goals. As a result, the new business revenue goal was doomed to fail before the year even started.

If it's early enough in the year, revise the goals now to make sure that all individuals are aligned with the big-picture vision. If it's too late for this year and you can't make a mid-year adjustment, make sure you and your team are on point during your planning for next year.

ARE YOUR SELLERS EXCITED TO COME TO WORK?

It was Wednesday morning when my son jumped up from his chair at breakfast proclaiming, "Hummmppp Day! It's going to be a great day!"

Intrigued by his pre-7am enthusiasm, I couldn't help but ask, "Evan, why is today going to be such a great day?" His response, "Because I have a science test and a math test. Also, today we're playing dodge ball in gym. Oh, and I get to see my teachers and friends!"

At 11 years old, Evan is able to look beyond the tests and get excited about the rest of the opportunities the day has to offer. Plus, I suspect, due to his competitive nature there might be a bit of anxiousness to test his skills. After all, he studied, so he might as well put it to good use.

Evan's comments got me thinking about my own school experience. There were times when I possessed the same enthusiasm about attending school, but more often than not, my most enjoyable memories of school result from an admiration of a great teacher or coach—someone who was relatable and a great leader. Someone who recognized a positive within that had yet to surface, and as a result they pushed me to grow by testing my limits.

Those same traits were consistent in individuals I considered to be mentors in the military, in college, and in my first years as a TV seller. It's a well-known fact that the first year in media sales isn't all peaches. There are rejections, self-doubt, and challenges that are unknown in other career paths. That's why it's so important for new, inexperienced sellers to secure the support and guidance of not only you, a TV sales manager, but also senior sellers who tend to have influence over the attitude of the staff. In short, the newbie needs to be taken under a wing until they're ready to fly on their own. Even then, they should be under close observation to keep the positive momentum going and to establish correct habits early in the career cycle.

From my observation, the best performing sales organizations are led by managers who create a culture that's competitive but fun and accountable but flexible and rewards driven—when deserved. These managers are sympathetic to the sales fight but continually challenge the preparedness of the team. These managers present a vision and a road map to goal achievement. Lastly, they lead by example and are "do as I do" *not* "do as I say" department heads.

It really comes down to managers being true *leaders* and creating a sales environment conducive to high morale and sales success. This is an environment that makes sellers excited to come to work despite any "tests" they may anticipate having to face throughout the day.

JACK WELCH'S 4 E'S OF LEADERSHIP

The iconic Jack Welch, in his best-selling book, *Winning!*, talks about the "4 E's of Leadership," his framework for hiring and promoting managers.

Sometimes the best accountability tool is a mirror. At the end of this reading, I encourage you to commit time to assess your "reflection in the mirror" and to conduct an honest observation of how your management performance matches up to Welch's 4 E's of Leadership characteristics.

1. ENERGY

Managers with *energy* move at 100mph in a 50mph world. They are naturally more productive, as their pace does not allow for lulls or long periods of down time. Year-to-year, single digit growth is not good enough for these types of television sales managers. They are comfortable with and many times even excited by stretch revenue goals.

High energy managers are generally more successful because they employ *planned abandonment*. They simplify the day by purging themselves of things that don't add value. This leaves energy for more productive selling and tasks that affect the bottom line.

2. ENERGIZERS

Professionals with this trait know how to rally a team. They lay out a vision, communicate it, and secure full buy-in. They are known as great recruiters and have an ability to bring out the best in sellers. Their enthusiasm for "the work" is contagious. Employees naturally want to follow these leaders.

Managers with the *energizer* trait genuinely care about individuals and their families. This is the type of supervisor who, at the station or cable office holiday party, will approach an AE's family bragging about the AE's special ability or performance.

These leaders are quick to spread deserved credit.

3. EDGE

Those individuals with *edge* are extremely competitive, but not overbearing. Change is not intimidating and they are the first in line ready to tackle a new opportunity.

Managers who possess edge are known for being direct communicators. They make eye contact and deliver the truth. They tend to tackle problems head-on and are quick to accept responsibility when something goes south on their watch.

Leaders with edge value speed in decision

making and are not afraid to say yes or no in uncomfortable circumstances. They're known for quick hiring, promotions, and firing decisions. Supervisors with edge have no patience for underperforming media sellers and often move swiftly to release the dead weight.

4. EXECUTE

From my observation, the television sales business is not short on saleable ideas. But sometimes we can be guilty of letting a great opportunity die, thanks to lack of execution. Without the ability to deliver results or execute, the other E's are of little value.

Managers who *execute* realize that productivity and activity are not one in the same. They are able to harness *energy* and *edge* into a payoff or positive result. Sales leaders who execute rarely miss budgets and they do their job better than anyone else in the same role before them.

So, how did you do? The good thing is that in this forum you aren't obligated to share your results with anyone. However, if you are unhappy after assessing where you fit in the 4 E's of Leadership, you still have time to make changes.

But, if you do nothing, beware. As author and speaker Giovanni Livera says, "No change, no change." What you choose to do now is up to you!

CHAPTER 2

COACHING TO WIN

Each person holds so much power within themselves that needs to be let out. Sometimes they just need a little nudge, a little direction, a little support, a little coaching, and the greatest things can happen. -Pete Carroll

WHAT TO DO AFTER CLOSING A BIG SALE

If you've known me for more than an hour, you know that I'm a die-hard The Ohio State football fan. I have been my whole life, all the way back to Woody Hayes and his hard-nosed *three yards and a cloud of dust* Buckeyes team.

Any of you who have the same passion about a sports team can imagine how excited I was during the 2015 National Championship when the underdog Buckeyes, led by Urban Meyer, lowered the boom on the Oregon Ducks.

There have been many sports history lessons

and analogies applied to our competitive business lives, which provide motivation and direction in areas like teamwork, performance, management, leadership, etc. So, I couldn't resist detailing a lesson from coach Urban Meyer's post-game interview as it relates to your sales team(s).

When Urban was asked, "What are you going to do now?" he didn't respond with the cliché, "I'm going to Disney World" (which is a great discussion on branding for another time). Instead, Urban looked into the camera and with great sincerity and passion said, "Tonight, I'm going to celebrate this win with this team—the guys I love. Tomorrow, we'll fly back to Columbus and get to work. We have a lot to do if we want to be here again next year!"

Think about that for a second. Ohio State had endured a second week loss that effectively knocked them out of playoff contention, plus a player suicide and season-ending injuries not only to the first string but also the second string quarterback. A run of seemingly insurmountable odds did little to stop the team from accomplishing their college football National Championship goal. Now, they're going to celebrate for less than a day before getting back to work. Who does that? In a word... *winners*.

Can you recall a time when an AE was walking the sales pit, mid-day, hootin' and hollerin' about the whale they just closed? They're excited and the celebration is warranted. In fact, a leader would jump right in and celebrate with the AE.

After, the average performing seller has their sights set on loafing for the rest of the day. Heck, because the sale was so much work, maybe they'll take the rest of the day off. As a manager, it's your job to encourage the AE to build on that positive momentum and finish the day trying to secure investments from other prospects.

You won't have to push a high-performing seller. They'll recognize that at that very moment their confidence is elevated and their "mojo" is about as positive as it's going to get. So after a short celebration and office "strut" they, just like Ohio State, will get right back to work. They're going to make a few more presentations, call a few more prospects—anything that involves asking for money. They're going to double-down on the positive attitude because to a high-performance seller, the euphoria of making a big sale, or in the case of Ohio State, a win, is a big enough draw that they want to experience the feeling as many times as possible and are willing to work tirelessly to get it.

A LETTER I HOPE YOUR AE'S DON'T WRITE

While working as a television group "corporate guy," I carried a *What Not To Do* case history folder. In this folder, I put ideas and samples that individuals, teams or stations should not repeat if they wanted to be successful. Call it a "learn from the example of others" resource.

One of my favorite *What Not To Do* examples is a letter with a Christmas advertising theme. The individual names and station have been blocked out to protect the guilty.

October 17, 2002

Dear ██████

I hope you're doing very well, and I hope life is good.

As you know, we haven't had any of your business since 1999. I would love the chance to get some of your budget for this Christmas.

Can you please call me back and allow me a twenty-minute presentation with you and██████. Perhaps I came on too strong on the phone with her on Thursday. I'll take the blame, but she was extremely negative and unwilling to even consider██████-TV. She was also unaware that we already knew each other and had done business before.

I presented a very hot idea that would only cost you $200 total! At the very least, look at this idea, which I'm enclosing.

In light of recent ratings and "overnight' technology that rates daily audiences for cable and WB, I urge you to have lunch with me and let's at least talk about who you are not reaching.

I hope you'll give me a call at ██████to arrange lunch or a meeting. ████ I'm "ok' with not getting bought by your store. But shouldn't we at least revisit things after three years?

All the best,

██████████

Wow! Is it any wonder the decision maker would not take this AE's phone call?

There are 190 words in this letter including *eighteen* references—nearly 10% of the writing—dedicated to "I," "me" or "we." In the sales process, sometimes an AE can get so focused on the sale that they become self-centric and forget about the client's goals. Less "me" and more "client" is always good to keep in mind when writing business correspondence.

How many clients trust, as the letter states, that your AE's can deliver a "hot" idea for $200? When something sounds too good to be true, guess what? It isn't true! It's best to leave that kind of statement out of a letter in order to protect your credibility.

Would you believe the AE author of this letter is now a very successful GSM at a boomer television station? That's proof that bad business etiquette can be corrected.

In case you're wondering how I would have written the letter... Very simply:

Mr. Potential Client,
  You've been missed!
  It's been nearly three years since our last opportunity to contribute to your advertising strategy. A lot has likely changed in the last three years—for both of us.
  Would it make sense to get together to discuss some of the changes and to talk about the possibility of exploring another marketing partnership? At the

very least, I'd like to share some regional minimal investment and giant return success stories that have the potential to substantially impact your holiday sales.

Do you have any room on your calendar the week of the 18th?

Sincerely, Winning AE

When I shared this story with Jim Doyle, he countered with a story about a corporate manager he knows who required his sales managers to get a copy of every single business letter and note that his AE's wrote. His managers learned three things when they did this:

#1 – The number of letters the team wrote went up! "We don't get what we expect, we get what we inspect!"

#2 – They (and probably you) had members of their team who couldn't write a clear business letter. This is big.

#3 – They had team members who could write clear letters, which were horrible selling letters. That's even bigger.

A LOW PRESSURE SALES CLOSING TECHNIQUE

After a long road trip I always look forward to arriving home, dropping the bags on the floor, and collecting hugs from my wife and our three kids. The conversation, after hugs, always begins with, "How was your trip?"

One night, upon my return home, our then 13-year-old daughter, Madison, skipped the "How was your trip?" question. In mid-hug she asked, "Are you excited to go to my music concert tomorrow night?"

What? Who even knew she was going to *be* in a music concert? Note the "<u>Are you excited</u> to go to..." structure of the question, instead of "<u>Do you want</u> to go to..." A 13-year old was attempting to sell me with an *assumptive* close!

The fact that I'm a sales teacher and trainer tells you that I've been around the sales block a few times but, for the life of me, there was no figuring out if Madison's assumptive close attempt was purposeful or by accident. (Note: could the concept have locked in? Maybe, as she had previously sat through hours of *DoyleOnDemand.com* edits!)

The assumptive closing technique is low pressure, natural, and simplified. Essentially, an AE is collecting agreeable confirmation, and is professionally guiding the client to a mutually beneficial win-win. It's as if the end result (we *will* be doing business together) is almost a foregone conclusion. Given the right conditions, it's one of the easiest closes to execute. Notice I said, "Given the right conditions." That's important for your sellers to understand. If there's pushback or a lack of agreement from a client during the presentation, it's a safe bet this is not the right condition for an assumptive close.

Those who lack confidence should also shy away from this close. Unfortunately, there are still AE's who have trouble when it's time to talk money in a presentation. I'm in near tears on sales calls when an AE stammers and stumbles over the "ask" and the potential sale gets railroaded.

Teach your sales pros to confidently address the money portion of the presentation. After the summary discussion, the monthly investment should appear and be addressed for just a few seconds. For example, with enthusiasm and showmanship, "Mr. Client, that's 324 commercials annually, a robust and tracked SEO campaign, and production of four commercials for a monthly investment of only $7,240." Your AE should not linger, but instead let the total sink in for not more than a few seconds before immediately moving on to the next page detailing timelines for creative and production.

In essence, without stating it, the message subtly conveyed from the AE to the client is, "This idea is so strong and will deliver a more-than-reasonable ROI, that I *assume* the money is not going to be an issue. As a result, we're now moving on to timelines."

Train your sales stars to use variations of this

assumptive closing question when discussing timelines: "Unless you have a conflict, we will schedule the production shoot on Thursday the 27th." If the client confirms the date, the AE has now gotten a sale. However, anything other than confirming a production date will result in the seller circling back into the presentation, digging deeper for the real objection, and trying alternative closes.

To finish my story, did Madison "assumptive close" me on going to her music concert? You bet she did! Who among us could look into their daughter's eyes—eyes that haven't been seen in a week—and tell her no? Maybe that look from a daughter should be called the *pulling on the heart-string* close.

ARE YOUR CLIENTS SUFFERING FROM ANTICIPOINTMENT?

My new favorite word is "anticipointment." On second thought, I'm not even sure it's a recognized word. TV news consultants use it to describe the disappointment when viewers are let down because they were anticipating something bigger. In any northern market, USA you can think of a station or cable channel's overhyped, sleeves-rolled-up coverage of the supposed *Snow Storm To End All Storms* that ultimately enters and leaves the area, quietly dropping only a few snowflakes. To the viewers who fought heavy traffic to grab the last milk on the near-empty supermarket shelves, this is *anticipointment*.

In the sales process, are your sellers guilty of anticipointment in negotiations with clients? In other words, do your AE's *over-promise* and *under-deliver*?

I remember well my days as a sales manager, spending hours in client offices, apologizing for an account executive who, in order to get the buy, committed to something with the client that we were unable to fulfill. The "what" that was committed to didn't matter. It could have been a rate, digital offering, commercial concept, placement, timeline, etc. In the end, the client had an expectation and we fell short.

How do you get a handle on sellers who seemingly can't say "no" to a client and consistently place you, the sales manager, in an uncomfortable position? You need to have repeated and clear communication on boundaries and limitations. Help the AE understand that "yes, we want business, but at some point there is a giant WIN for the client but only a small, unacceptable win for our team." Help your sellers understand that it's okay to say "no." If the client persists, your AE should respond with, "No... but." As in, "*No*, we cannot get you into Thursday prime time for that rate, *but* we can find the same number of points at that rate in access

36

programming."

Your sales stars need to explain the return on investment for client anticipointment resulting from unrealistic expectations. Please train your team to recognize that high-ticket items are best suited for an ROI model. Telling a client they need to sell 189,326 candy bars to break even next month does nothing to advance the sale. However, an attorney suddenly becomes interested when he understands the advertising has to deliver *only* 4 more cases a month to get a 2 to 1 return.

Sometimes, media sellers will make promises on offerings they don't understand. As a result, they may be surprised when confronted about a client's anticipointment. This happens a lot when AE's are trying to fulfill digital sales demands. Make sure your training addresses all the in's and out's of your digital offerings. If a seller still doesn't understand, have the digital sales manager, or a more knowledgeable rep, accompany the seller on calls until he or she thoroughly understands the products, assuming the seller still has potential.

Lastly, creative discussions sometimes give way to anticipointment. A sales rep may promise that the "be all, end all" creative idea is on its way, but when presented, the idea falls short of the client's thought process. This happens when an overly enthusiastic rep does a poor job of managing anticipation and the client expects dancing bears and helicopters. Instead of AE's promising that a soon-to-be-delivered idea will solve all the world's issues, they need to learn to present with realistic and credible phrases. Doing so will temper unrealistic expectations and remove client anticipointment.

Don't Let "What Ifs" Get In The Way Of Opportunity

The year was 1984 and she stood out in the crowd like a neon light in a dark room. To me, she was the most beautiful girl in our little town of almost 15,000 residents. Who was I kidding? She was the most beautiful thing I had seen in my whole life which, to that point, had consisted of about 16 years of living! The thought of approaching her scared me to death. After all, we lived on opposite sides of the tracks. She was book smart and went to a private catholic school, while I spent time avoiding all that a public high school education had to offer, unless it involved some kind of athletic endeavor. I knew I had to speak to her, but hesitated. That voice—you know, the one between the ears that has the power to stop all forward momentum—kept saying, "What if?" What if she doesn't talk to me? What if she's not interested? What if she's already dating someone else? Thankfully, the want to meet Bridget overcame the nagging what if's and, as of this writing, we've been married for over 22 years. But, *what if* I didn't muster up the courage to speak to her all those years ago?

Let's shift gears and talk about another love story. It's about a love of television sales and the desire for an ever-increasing commission check. No doubt, many of the sellers on your team fit that description. But despite their good intentions and want for improvement, do you ever catch them unknowingly asking:

- What if the client gets upset because we asked for too much money?
- What if they've already spent their budget?
- What if I interrupt them while they're meeting with customers?
- What if the last digital campaign with us didn't work?

In a Jim Doyle & Associates Leaders Edge tele-seminar, self-discipline strategist and best-selling author Rory Vaden (www.roryvaden.com) stated, "The reason we procrastinate is that we're trying to circumvent paying the price."

So, when you hear your stars peppering their progress updates with "what ifs," they're telegraphing fear. The what if gives them an excuse to delay the inevitable or, worse yet, not make the call at all. As a manager and leader, you need to guide the AE back to a level of confidence that will encourage them to make the client call. Statements like, "What if they had record sales resulting from our digital campaign?" or "Let's not make the decision for the client, let's give them the courtesy of giving us a yes or no," are great conversation starters that will move fearful thinking back in the right direction.

As managers, are we sometimes guilty of the "what ifs?" Maybe you justify preferred treatment with "between the ears" statements like, "What if I push our #1 biller too hard and they leave?" or "What if I fire the dead weight and can't find a replacement?"

When these thoughts enter your mind, reverse the question to get your thinking moving in a positive direction. For example, "What if I push our #1 biller and they set an all-time new revenue record?" or "What if I don't fire the dead weight? What negative effect will that have on the attitude of the rest of the staff?"

Practicing these negative to positive statement reversals is important because opportunity in some form presents itself every day. The opportunities are ours for the taking, assuming we don't let "what ifs" get in the way!

MEASURING YOUR SALES PROMOTIONS

There's a difference between a promotion and a

sales promotion. Promotions, in general, should advance the public's consumption or use of the channel, whether in minutes spent viewing or online. A *sales* promotion, however, has the added burden of delivering revenue. Both versions are necessary, but smart television managers under budget scrutiny are finding ways to create more sales promotion opportunities.

There are *four* measurements to consider when determining if a sales promotion opportunity is going to be successful:

1. **Does it make money?**
2. **Does it extend the station / channel / media outlet program or online brand?**
3. **Will it increase the client's investment with you?**
4. **Are the viewer's interests being met?**

1. Does it make money? We can easily eliminate "added value" black holes from the sales promotion category. AE's may argue that the client received a free promotion resulting from an increased share or extra money spent on your medium. No. This is not a sales promotion.

In order to be considered a successful sales promotion, there has to be a charge to the client for participation, resulting in a positive cash balance *after* subtracting all expenses. Any other scenario is considered simply a promotion and does not immediately contribute cash to the sales effort.

2. Does it extend the station / channel / media outlet, program or online brand? If you cannot directly relate an uptick in viewing or digital consumption to a promotion, then it does not meet the criteria for advancing your brand. A great event will drive traffic to a client, while simultaneously driving eyeballs to your channel or website. A client supplying prizes for a "watch and win" will not get as much traffic as a client whose stores are "register to win" locations. For a true win-win, consider client locations for registration and then announce multiple winners over multiple days on-air.

3. Will it increase the client's investment with you? Policing this measurement is a number one priority for sales managers. Don't let AE's play the shell game by lowering commercial rates and then applying the excess to a sales promotion. Further, the cost of a sales promotion should be incremental above the client's previous annual investment. Positioning for "no increase" or "flat" investments has a negative revenue impact on ever escalating budgets.

4. Are the viewers' interests being met? A successful sales promotion means correct logos, meeting all deadlines, and making sure all the "i's" are dotted and the "t's" are crossed. A full explanation or even a dry run with all of your office and client participants is insurance against disappointed viewers and winners.

A mid-market station's flat screen sales promotion contest flopped when the station gave certificates to winners to take to the client to pick up their shiny new flat screens. The client made the mistake of not stocking the sets and told winners they would have to wait 4 to 6 weeks for another shipment. This was two weeks before the Super Bowl! The winners were not happy. There is no way of knowing how many potential "upsells" this client lost.

SALES SHORTCUTS LEAVE MONEY ON THE TABLE

I want to alert you to a topic that may exist among your sales team and you might not even know it. The reason it's not on your radar is because your sellers are still closing business. You might even be proud that your team is pacing ahead of last year's new business and local direct revenue. But, unless you correct what I'm about to discuss, your revenue victories may be short-lived.

Consistently in my visits to stations and media outlets, I see sellers present to a client and then watch as the team celebrates a *big* annual agreement close. Many times, in mental post-analysis, it occurs to me that (for example) the celebrated $60K close is maybe $50K short of what should have been the full potential of the sale. In other words, the *big* ($60K) sale could have been *bigger* ($110K), but the Account Executive took "shortcuts" in the sales process, leaving dollars on the table!

Many of these shortcut mistakes start during the client diagnosis conversation. Sellers avoid an in-depth business "dig" and as a result miss-call a client's differentiator, growth opportunity or, worse yet, they make assumptions about the client's business. During one of my stops, a not-for-profit said "yes" to an annual contract and then elatedly told the AE and LSM how surprised he was at the affordability of the station proposal. He was now going to be able to use a $138,000 county government grant to support *other* advertising! Wow! That would have been good info to know *before* the presentation!

Sometimes shortcuts are taken during the creation of the presentation. I've seen Account Executives accidentally leave wrong business names on slides. This mistake takes the "custom" out of customized. I uncomfortably watch AE's "wing it." They don't take the time to review the material, don't understand reach and frequency, or cannot elaborate on the testimonials included in the presentation. Even worse are the one-sided presentations—a big win for the station or cable office, but little or no-win for the advertiser—and which do little to address the client's needs. Often, these types of proposals have been shoved together at the last second with the AE claiming a lack of time. Unfortunately, in my observation, time is not the issue. These kinds of shortcuts result from a lack of effort.

Would you believe that senior account executives take more shortcuts than unseasoned AE's? Why? I'm not sure, but I suspect senior AE's feel like they've been to the dance before. Maybe they get tired with the process and begin to overlook details. Ultimately, they don't know what they don't know. This is where you, as the sales manager, need to get involved.

You have to work with these senior sellers to help them understand the big picture. Don't be surprised if you get push-back, because they are closing contracts. It's your role to help them understand that the situation is not one of closing but more about missed opportunity.

This senior seller discussion is crucial for the future of your entire sales team. If left unchecked, newer AE's begin to mimic the sales styles of the veterans and, before long, you have a whole team of short cutters and lots of client money sitting on the table ready to fortify your competitors' budgets.

DON'T LET YOUR TEAM PRACTICE SALES PROFILING

They are lying in wait nearly every week as I roll my luggage through Atlanta's Delta Terminal A.

Their job is to "yell out" to passing travelers. They have barely a one-sentence chance to say something clever enough to entice passers-by to stop their rush to the gate to discuss the benefits of signing up for a Delta American Express credit card. The incentive to prospects? Thirty thousand Delta frequent flyer miles.

On one particular trip, my gate was within earshot of the Delta credit card desk. I had a front row vantage point to observe the entire sales process—from how they prospected to their presentation, objections, and closing. This team of sellers is good. They also have very thick skin as theirs is a job of rejection. For what I guess is every fifty or so "no's," they'd get just one "yes."

But, for the first time I noticed that every seller was making a huge mistake. They were *sales profiling*. That's right. They were allowing individuals in business attire a free pass while they continued to pitch casual or non-business dressed prospects.

Where is it written that everyone in an airport wearing a suit, sport coat or tie *is not* interested in extra frequent flyer miles? To be fair, I travel so much it would take more than a 30,000 mile offer to entice me to get another credit card. But maybe if business professionals were stopped and engaged they would switch if they discovered something advantageous—like better interest rates.

"Give the prospect the courtesy to tell you no," is a line I repeated often as a sales manager. My feeling was that there are hidden losses when one gets caught up in sales profiling. This only happens because without client consultation, the seller assumes they know better. They "think" there's no potential, instead of giving the prospect the courtesy of answering the question.

How does one know that the non-profit is due a big dollar grant that will result in a huge marketing campaign? Or, why does a junior AE have success with a furniture store that a senior AE said is a waste of time to prospect? Help your team understand that a *one* location dry cleaner, restaurant, auto dealer, etc., is one bank loan away from *three* locations. But, in order to be "in the know" for these opportunities, your sellers will need to speak with the prospect instead of pre-judging.

It should be noted that I understand the value of time vs. effort and am in no way stating your AEs should chase $200 accounts. There's a minimum investment threshold and if a prospect can't afford it, your sellers should move on and find another up. But the discovery of the ability to afford or not afford is not possible if your team subscribes to sales profiling.

I Tried TV And It Didn't Work

"I tried TV and it didn't work," the furniture store

owner sternly stated. Upon further conversation, the prospect explained to me that she had felt taken advantage of when she previously invested in a few of our competing media's special holiday television advertising packages that didn't work. This business owner's perception of most media reps is that they are unreliable and self-serving and, as a result, are *not* to be trusted with her marketing dollars.

How would your sellers respond to a client's similar concern? I suspect the conversation would circle around some form of, "What channels were used or what was in the commercial?"

Here's a tip. The next move from your AE should be one of trying to establish trust, and simultaneously, distancing themselves from the bad experience. Anything short of "repositioning" is a shaky answer. What is repositioning? It's the ability to move the buyer's memory of a negative experience to a positive anticipatory thought process. The prospect needs to think, "This rep is different."

Train your AE's to understand that repositioning begins with a simple "clearing house" statement to set the foundation before the relationship can move forward. As an example, *"Ms. Prospect, it sounds like a television sales rep, long previous to me, may have been looking out for themselves and maybe had their own best interest at heart.*"

The AE should continue to establish a connection with something like, "*I wish I'd met you before your bad media experience because you would understand that there are indeed reps who take a genuine interest in the success of your business.*"

A statement like, "*I appreciate that you will not let your negative experience reflect poorly on me at the outset of our relationship,*" helps your sellers establish a loose agreement of terms.

The final statement—the wrap-up—should contain some air of credibility. "*My clients are long-term partners; businesses that continually depend on me, month after month and year after year, to help dramatically grow their sales. I'm not into one-time closes. We'll discuss expectations and establish benchmarks for a solid return on your investment. Does it make sense for us to continue our conversation?*"

If the client still doesn't respond favorably, it's time to get another up!

AN OBSERVATION ON TRAINING

Every couple of years, I find myself anxious to take in the incredible depth of Olympic television coverage, not just for the many competitions but also for the stories that accompany the athletes. Many have sacrificed and have overcome some form of adversity in pursuit of a life dream for that very Olympic moment.

Each athlete's commitment is derived from a belief that success could be within their grasp as long as they stay committed to a regimen of hard work and relentless *training*.

Michael Phelps, United States swimming Olympic gold medalist in 2004, 2008, and 2012 summarized his experience: "I think that everything is possible as long as you put your mind to it and put the work and time into it." Isn't that true of anything in life? Sports? Business? Marriage?

As a broadcasting or cable leader and coach, are you preparing your sales team? Are you giving them the tools necessary to perform at the highest sales levels? Are you consistently *teaching* and *training* them on the basics of sales?

Too often, we hear horror stories of managers verbally unloading on the team because of their lack of sales. Some of these managers are too busy to go on sales calls with the Account Executives, and training within the media outlet is nonexistent. In these cases, should anyone be surprised when budgets are missed and staff turnover is high?

If you take a look at our company website (www.jimdoyle.com), you'll see the statement: *We make you money, we make you better!* We are a sales teaching and training company. Why do we think training is so important? Because the typical broadcasting or cable sales staff churns nearly *thirty* percent of their team annually. Think about that for a second. How much time, effort, and money are wasted trying to keep a sales staff together and productive?

To reach all levels of ability on your staff, consider a formal training system in addition to your station staff-conducted training. Meetings led by AE's stick out as some of the best. Keep the sales meetings on the same day each week. Incorporate music, food, video, guest speakers, and different meeting locations. While creating an annual training calendar, ask the AE's for topics they'd like to explore.

Great managers understand the value of consistent, "on the calendar," thought-provoking training. They view sales training as a necessary time and money investment as opposed to an interruption to the sales day. These managers make training fun and something that the Account Executives anticipate instead of dread. They know a well-trained staff is more successful. Somehow, budgets get made, morale improves, and your team becomes the model that makes competitors nervous.

TEN SIGNS AN ACCOUNT EXECUTIVE IS DYING

Many years ago, as a still relatively new local

sales manager, I was trying to arrive at a firing decision. Then, on a managers' conference call, I received absolute clarity on the situation after hearing our company President and CEO, Dan Sullivan, say, "When expectation turns to hope, it's time to make a change." The point being, when an AE is falling short in performance, "hoping" does nothing to help them get better at selling. It takes action, typically in the form of examples, mentoring, training, and accountability. When all is exhausted in these areas, the "change" needed may be a freeing of the non-performer for better suited opportunities.

For many, firing someone is a very difficult and emotional event, but doing so is necessary to the process of "weeding" out a staff as you build toward a team of optimum performers. As television sales managers, we have to assume some responsibility for identifying when account executives are headed for a fall. It is important to identify when they're "dying" early in the process, so there's time for a revamp or correction.

Chris Cunningham, a former sales manager at one of our partner stations, was a manager who understood the importance of this weeding out. After attending one of our Sales Manager's High Performance Boot Camps, he decided to dig a little deeper into this topic and created the below chart.

TEN SIGNS AN ACCOUNT EXECUTIVE IS DYING

1. They are in the office more than they are out with clients
2. They are resistant to "firing" accounts that are not going anywhere
3. They stop being a team player and start to worry about others' business instead of their own
4. They reduce themselves to the "minimum" number of calls per day
5. They don't know the name of the decision-makers on their account list
6. When a sales manager rides with them, they can't locate the client's business
7. They know nothing about the client BEFORE they go in
8. They come in right on time or late, and leave at the close of business
9. They stop listening to their clients and assume they know more than the business owner
10. They become complacent and don't want to adapt to the new methods and utilize the tools available (mobile, digital, consulting, research, multiple platforms, etc.)

If you have an AE for whom you find yourself answering in the affirmative on many of the above questions, the time for action is now.

CHAPTER 3

MANAGING FOR MAXIMUM PERFORMANCE

Management is nothing more than motivating other people. -Lee Iacocca

PROPERLY MANAGE TOP PERFORMERS TO AVOID WORKPLACE HEARTBURN

You can likely recall that sinking feeling in your gut when one of your sales stars unexpectedly tendered their resignation. Or, maybe you hired away a superstar from a competitor and a few short weeks later you determined the "superstar" was less than stellar in your organization. Enter again, that sinking feeling in your gut.

The key to avoiding that workplace heartburn is to understand how to manage a "top performer." Many times these stars end up leaving or losing their sales energy because they're mismanaged or misunderstood.

Many years ago, as the general manager of a TV station, I listened to our GSM complain that our new hire of *four* months had all but stopped his local direct and new business sales effort. It had been a real "get" when we lured this AE away from a competitor. He was extremely well-respected and one of the top local direct sellers in the market. Upon investigation, I discovered that the GSM had rewarded our new hire's billing efforts with regional agency accounts. The AE complained that the accounts required a lot of time and maintenance— time that he could be out on the street seeing local clients. Once the GSM re-assigned the agency accounts, the star AE was happy and almost immediately started pumping in local direct and new business revenue.

Engaging the seller and asking "why?" was key to heading off a resignation. Where is it written that every AE has to handle a certain amount of agency accounts? By dropping that requirement for this star, the AE was happy and the station's local direct billing benefited tremendously.

I've always been a believer that one should treat their top performers differently. Please don't misunderstand my statement. I am not suggesting that rules don't apply and the inmates should run the asylum. Instead, when managing stars, you should set loose parameters of accountability, let them know where the limitations are, and allow them to do what they do best—sell. Ask them for input on big projects and get their buy-in, as their effort will likely determine the team's sales success.

Believe it or not, money is not typically the primary motivator for top sellers. They know that if they continue their high level of performance the money will come. Generally, their motivations are achievement, personal growth, recognition, respect, and big-picture guidance.

HANDLING AN UNCOMFORTABLE MEETING

The meeting was an uncomfortable one-on-one with an employee. After they had screwed up, it was on me to walk them through the repercussions of their actions and provide the next steps to improve the situation.

If you're like me, sometimes the build-up to these types of encounters weighs heavily on the brain. But from my experience, a little organization and preparation will go a long way to keeping both you and the employee focused on the topic at hand and help provide clarity in your communication.

The first step to conducting these meetings is to get all of the pertinent information on paper. This will serve as your discussion reference point and ensure that emotion doesn't get in the way, potentially derailing the intent of the meeting. Typically, this consists of bullet points of *facts* you wish to convey that are relevant to the situation.

As you may remember from Stan Freberg's *Dragnet* parodies, "Nothing but the facts ma'am." There's no room for gossip and innuendo on this sheet.

When conducting these sit-downs, I have found it effective to very quickly define on the front end *why* the meeting is taking place. Beating around the bush adds confusion to the conversation as the employee continues to guess where you're headed with the conversation. You might consider opening the meeting with something like, "Tom, you really screwed up. But today's meeting is not about firing you. Instead, today is about making sure you understand the issue so that we don't find ourselves in this situation again."

You should supply detailed next steps. However, if you don't have buy-in from the employee on the next steps then don't expect the situation to change. That's why you may choose to encourage the employee to go home and sleep on the discussion then come back with some tangible next step thoughts the following day. This employee participation, regardless of whether or not you've guided them in the process, ensures the employee has "skin in the game," which results in a much higher correction success rate.

The meeting should end with two questions: 1) Is there any confusion or do I need to clarify any of the points we discussed today? and 2) Have I missed anything?

With these two questions you are confirming the communication is clear and that the employee is satisfied with the discussion. This information will come in handy in the off chance the issue does not get fixed and you find it necessary to build a file for possible termination.

The biggest mistake in this process is waiting. What I mean is, because these meetings can be uncomfortable, some managers may be reluctant to quickly address the topic with an employee. These managers turn their heads, almost acting as though there is no issue. In time, the "it will go away" has turned into a giant snowball issue.

Don't wait. The employees are counting on you to lead. Great leaders understand how a small action can turn into a cancer. They act swiftly and decisively to correct a problem. They don't blame corporate for lack of action. They hold themselves accountable and, as a result, the team is held accountable. Everyone understands where the lines are drawn.

A TIERED SALES PROMOTION STRATEGY

How good is your Creative Services Director? Do they ever say "no" to AE's? From my observation, the best Creative Services Directors possess a strong backbone. They aren't afraid to deny a request. However, they don't say "no" out of spite. Instead, their reluctance to honor every AE client "ask" is in defense of the brand and protection of their precious promotional inventory, which ultimately helps drive ratings momentum.

I have no idea how the expectation of "added value" originated. But I do know that many clients, predominantly agencies, won't hesitate to tack on added value requests as a condition of the station or cable outlet accepting a buy. Then, assuming all the free on-air ID's have been passed out, your AE's will march down the hall to see the Creative Services Director and ask, "What added value can you give my client?"

To prevent these instances, it would be beneficial to adopt a Tiered Sales Promotion strategy to make nice with the Creative Services Department, your clients, and viewers. Creative Services will enjoy the adoption of this plan because it defines their inventory commitments. Clients will like the fact that you have the year laid out with defined opportunities and levels of participation depending upon their incremental investments. No longer will your company look like a NASCAR vehicle with single client promos, click to wins, call now, etc., at every break. This will please viewers. These types of promotions get rolled up into bigger promos with multiple client participants, which frees up airtime for ratings builders like episodics or programming promotions.

Here's how a tiered system of sales promotions

works.

In conjunction with your Creative Services Director, list all promotions in the last year. Then determine which promotions included, needed or were made better with client participation. Lastly, select the promotions that can be expanded to make them bigger and better, and then cross off the ones that are no longer relevant. Now you're ready to "tier" your sales promotion effort.

Tier 1: These are large scale, big effort, big money, multi-month promotions. They're not programming driven. These types of promotions expand your brand and impact community awareness. Sponsorship includes multiple clients, typically the highest incremental spenders. Examples: College scholarship giveaways, high school sports tie-ins, or major charity efforts like Coats for Kids, Habitat for Humanity or Breast Cancer Awareness.

Tier 2: This category is for medium investment clients. These promotions are easier to execute vs. Tier 1 and can be community impactful but still multi-client inclusive, with an emphasis on forced viewing. Examples: Watch to win a trip to Italy and a Vespa scooter and pizza for a year, hands on a car giveaway, or an on-air viewer wedding proposal.

Tier 3: These promotions are the easiest to execute. Their on-air or digital timeline is the shortest of all three categories. More often than not they're created as a result of client demand and, like Tier 1 and 2, include multiple clients. Examples: Advance movie screenings, registers to win, and ticket giveaways via on-air and Internet.

SEARCHING FOR A MOVIE WITH A FEW CHEAP LAUGHS

It was a rainy Saturday afternoon; a day to steal a few uninterrupted hours on the couch, vegging with the television remote and surfing for nothing in particular, maybe a comedy—a movie that wouldn't take a lot of brain power to view.

The On Demand button didn't disappoint as I discovered a Vince Vaughn movie called *Unfinished Business*. He was great in *Wedding Crashers* so I figured risking $5.95 and 93 minutes was worth the gamble. Besides, I wasn't looking for a life lesson story line, just some weekend comfort viewing.

The movie begins with Vince closing a big sale then finding out from his sales manager that his commission is going to be cut 5%. He's so upset that he quits on the spot and declares he is starting his own company to compete against his previous employer. Did I mention he sells metal shavings?

Two misfits join Vince to round out the new company and they spend the rest of the movie trying to secure their financial futures by pursuing a "hand shake" from a huge account.

Vince finds out that his previous employer is also pitching the huge account and the movie takes on a comedic David vs. Goliath twist. Just when it appears all is lost, Vince uses an inside the company "gatekeeper" relationship to get to the elusive highest decision maker.

To find out the ending, you'll have to watch the movie for yourself. However (possible spoiler alert here), I think you already know the likely outcome when one salesperson is talking to a *non-decision maker* and the other salesperson is talking to the *decision maker*.

Too many times I see sellers who are content with presenting to prospects with no decision making authority. It's a comfortable move with minimal objections. These AE's then report back to their sales managers that everything looks positive and they should have a "yes" any day now. Time passes, the shine begins to wear off the penny, and the expected "yes" turns into a "no." Soon after, the prospect's commercial is seen on a competitor's channel.

If this scenario sounds familiar, it's time to remind your sales team of the value of getting to the ultimate decision maker—someone who can say "yes" when everyone else says "no." There's no possible reason that your sellers should rest the fate of the sale in the hands of an intermediary.

Getting to the decision maker can sometimes be

a difficult task, one that may involve a general-to-general call or corraling various relationships at multiple levels. Or it may require coincidental run-ins when defenses are down, outside the prospect's office. If all is lost, the final step may be a heart-to-heart with the intermediary to plead for their assistance for an introduction to the decision maker. Make sure your AE's state the WIFM (what's in it for them) clearly to the gatekeeper and how they'll be portrayed as the hero in the scenario.

Anything short of a plan to get in front of the ultimate decision maker is wasted time and wasted effort, as I was unexpectedly reminded of when searching for a movie with a few cheap laughs.

MOVING ON IS NOT GIVING UP

It was the 2012 BCS title college football game where #2 ranked Alabama, led by coach, Nick Saban, was manhandling #1 ranked Notre Dame so definitively that by the end of the second quarter, nearly everyone, including the Irish head coach, Brian Kelly, was conceding the game was over.

At halftime, when a sideline reporter asked Kelly about second half adjustments, Kelly responded, "Maybe Alabama doesn't come back in the second half? It's all Alabama. I mean we can't tackle 'em right now." Whether you liked the answer or not, you have to give Kelly credit for being honest with a national audience.

As a television sales manager, are you as honest as Brian Kelly was? In other words, when all parties understand that a sales effort has hit a dead end, do you push forward with the agenda or are you willing to stop, cut your losses, and go find another "up"?

Some of you are probably thinking that stopping the process is giving up. When we're younger we're taught that giving up is a sign of weakness. Giving up *is not* what I'm suggesting. The point here is that we cannot sell everyone. When the sales process is exhausted and the answer is still "no," then maybe it is time to move on and find another prospect. Moving on is not giving up. Instead, it's understanding defeat. You have no chance of "winning" the sale and, as a result, you're making a decision that your time is better served finding another prospect. The value in this lesson is the "experience learned" that will help your sales stars close business down the road.

In the post-game press conference, Brian Kelly provided no game analysis. As difficult as it may have been, he was able to find the silver lining in Notre Dame's outmatched and unwinnable situation. "Our guys needed to see what it looked like to play a championship team." He continued, "The best thing about this experience is it creates fire—it creates a fuel for the guys staying here and the guys leaving, and everybody here... everybody here tonight... will be better because of it."

Brian Kelly was able to admit defeat, explain how he values the lesson learned, and set forward thinking thoughts for the team's next season of opportunity. As television sales managers, we could learn a lot from the way Brian Kelly handled himself after that game.

WHY DO AE'S HATE POLITICAL ADVERTISING?

Have you heard this political advertising joke? How many Brinks trucks does it take to haul a TV station's political revenue to the bank? Always one more!

Television political advertising revenue continues to set records with each election cycle. In conversations with senior broadcasting leaders, nearly all have admitted they knew the political windfalls were going to continue to grow but not at the levels they are seeing today. In these times, not even a crystal ball can help with the inventory management in the weeks leading up to oversell. When it comes to the clearance and rate dance, many managers are truly faced with "packing 10 pounds of sugar into a 5-pound bag."

I remember, as a sales manager, making a *huge* mistake by sprinting to the sales pit, loudly celebrating a new "all time" record rate in Monday

Night Football, courtesy of the state gubernatorial race. The NSM and LSM joined me in celebration, while the AE's sat silent. The AE's were silent because each had nearly two pages of pre-emptions on their desk, with little hope of getting them back into the system. Translation—the station was getting paid while the AE's were losing money. Plus, they had the extra burden of conducting daily damage control with upset clients. Does this story sound familiar?

I'm pretty sure that if you're reading this book, you're a "for profit" entity. Please allow me to make it very clear that I am all for taking the higher rate and pre-empting the lower. However, when pre-empts begin to stack up, you'll need a dollar-shift plan because the tight inventory situation compounds when AE's try to "make good" on their pre-empts at the same or "close to" rate, while political orders continue to arrive. In these instances, you need to condition AE's to think beyond the thirty-second commercial to save the money.

Here are some thoughts you might consider to help your AE's find a home for their clients' hard earned advertising dollars—away from the thirty-second battleground:

1. Move the dollars to one of your digital channels.
2. Create a social media contest to push

business leads.
3. Consider a digital or mobile campaign.
4. Dust off or create new website video pre-roll opportunities.
5. Move the client money to sponsorships with billboards.
6. Consider re-editing client commercials into five- and ten-second versions.
7. Utilize onscreen graphics to create client "bugs" to be dropped into programming, news, and time/temp updates.
8. Produce lower third programming "squeeze backs" with client video and/or audio identification.

Ultimately, in the heat of inventory demand, clients will appreciate your effort. It's a pretty good bet they're experiencing market wide pre-emptions. Another good bet is that you may be the *only* media outlet communicating with the client and trying to help them stay visible and vocal during the political window.

I want to close with something that, during heavy political spending, made a difference in the morale of our sales stars. As a side note, this did not happen until after that experience with "silent AE's with pre-empts" mentioned earlier. We created a commission "pool" (a couple of points from the political windfall total) that was then shared among the sales staff. Each AE received a percentage of the pool, equal to their average percentage to total local billing in a non-political window. Doing so provided the AE's with a sense of relief and allowed them to work ahead on December and the coming year, without fear of ending the 4th quarter with personal financial loss.

Please, *do not* tell your corporate boss, "John Hannon said I need political money to pay AE's." I was simply sharing the voice of my experience!

So, enjoy the extra political revenue while it lasts, but don't forget to take time to plan a strategy for sales revenue success before the Brinks truck pulls away from your office.

Don't Count Your Political Money Before It Arrives

Continuing our discussion of potential political year pitfalls, I remember a time when, as the general manager of a television station in Dayton, Ohio, the final touches had just been approved on the station's annual budget, and the general consensus was that we were going to easily blow past our revenue budget.

Thanks to the luck of being in Ohio, we were going to be the benefactors of never-before-seen levels of political advertising dollars. It seemed that every office from President, federal and state, local commissions, mayors, etc., was going to be on the ballot. Additionally, in this particular year, the Republicans were concerned about the growing support of the Ohio Democrats. My "in the know" friend at the local Republican headquarters office had informed our station's sales managers that Ohio had always been a red state and the party was prepared to spend whatever dollars were needed to ensure a victory over the Democrats. It was common knowledge that a loss of Ohio in November meant a loss of the presidency for the party. For good measure, I decided to add the Brink's truck phone number to my office speed dial!

During budget planning, we raised March through May budgets to account for the primary election. There was no cause for alarm when we started falling short of our 2nd quarter projections, as we were certain the political windfall that typically hit the books mid-August through the November election would more than make up for the Q2 billing shortfall.

By September, the market inventory was nearly sold-out. Virtually every day part on our station had established a new rate high. In retrospect, we should have been nicer when happily informing local advertisers, many of whom had been loyal to us around the year, that there was no commercial availability. Our confident sales swagger collapsed like a house of cards when the seemingly impossible happened—

cancellations.

We were unconcerned after receiving the first few cancellations. After all, political order revisions, cancellations, and rebooks were not uncommon. However, market-wide cancellations started hitting because, for the first time in history, the Grand Old Party decided to raise the white flag and cede Ohio to the Democrats. The Republican strategy had changed literally overnight and as a result multiple *millions* of Republican advertising dollars were leaving Ohio, headed for television stations in the southeast. To add insult to injury, the Democrats decided to follow suit with their own cancellations. After all, why waste a ton of money in a state the Republicans were fleeing?

Don't kid yourself when it comes to holding a political advertiser to your *two-week* cancellation policy. If, during the course of the year, you let anyone out of a contract before *two* weeks, then you must do the same for a political race. Additionally, it's unlikely that you're going to be successful if everyone else is caving on the *two-week* cancellation. You have no leverage.

Panic is an understatement for our post-cancellations market environment. Inventory was now wide open with no one to buy. Many advertisers, choosing not to compete with political clutter, had cut out September through November television advertising from their budget. Many more had decided to invest their money in competing mediums. All had short memories and were still recovering from the bruises of a seller's market only a few weeks prior.

The stations were now in a game of "the lowest rate wins," which often results in scenarios like 90% of inventory sold at 65% of revenue budget. This is *not* exactly a revenue model for success.

It took the market about *four* months before the rates recovered to numbers that gave stations an outside shot at making budgets in the new year. The whole experience stands out as an invaluable career-teaching tool.

It's unlikely you could replace all lost political money, but you can take some definitive steps as insurance, should political revenue unexpectedly disappear from your pacing:

- Be creative to convert commercial dollars to non-spot dollars. Find a way to make sure key clients don't go dark or move *your* dollars to another medium because they fear rate inflation and political "noise."
- Utilize squeeze backs, menu lineups, ID's, client bugs and sponsorships as a way to keep clients in front of viewers.
- Review your inventory status daily to track trends for political volume slow down.
- Stay extremely close to political planners or local party chairpersons for advance notice

on strategy changes.

- Make deposits with key clients. Alert them to on-air opportunities or open inventory that may increase their exposure. Doing so will make your station stand out among the competition when the political dust clears.
- Assign the responsibility of monitoring competing stations' political buys to someone. Doing so is much easier now that all stations must list this activity on their websites, and the exercise will help confirm market estimates or individual station positioning.

Warning: It's imperative that all your team members who are responsible for the political buys in your outlet are aware of current political advertising laws and regulations. A few consulting firms are now conducting post-election political file audits and are making a nice living pocketing a commission on cash credits due candidates.

STOP GIVING PARTICIPATION TROPHIES

Pittsburgh Steeler James Harrison posted on Instagram his intent to give back his sons' sports "participation" trophies:

"I came home to find out that my boys received two trophies for nothing, participation trophies! While I am very proud of my boys for everything they do and will encourage them till the day I die,

*these trophies will be given back until they EARN a real trophy. I'm sorry that I'm not sorry for believing that everything in life should be earned and I'm not about to raise two boys to be men by making them believe that they are entitled to something just because they tried their best... cause sometimes your best is not enough, and that should drive you to want to do better... not cry and whine until somebody gives you something to shut up and keep you happy." (#*harrisonfamilyvalues)

At the risk of showing my age, participation trophies did not exist when I was younger. We played the sport of the season—football in the fall, basketball in the winter and baseball in the spring and summer. If your team didn't finish 1st, 2nd or maybe 3rd, you went home *without* hardware but benefitted from a lesson in humility.

That was the same with school awards. There was no class participation certificate. One either worked hard, got good grades and made the honor roll, or one didn't.

I'm not sure when or how these awards for merely participating became the norm. Can you imagine if you gave sales bonuses to your AE's for simply showing up for work? That would be ludicrous and counter-productive to the positive momentum cultures and revenue machines that sales managers work so hard to create.

From my experience, the best performers—the

stars and leaders—are successful because they have faced some form of adversity and have been able to overcome the setbacks. They learned from their experiences. Maybe they thought they were good only to be surprised that someone else was much better. That drive, the mere focus of self-betterment to improve and excel beyond the competition, is what makes these individuals so good. They dream of the trophy that no one else gets. They appreciate a world where someone will win and, as a result, someone else will lose.

James Harrison didn't get a college scholarship for football. He was a Kent State walk-on that went undrafted in 2002. He pursued his NFL dream by playing a year in NFL Europe before joining the Baltimore Ravens. The Ravens cut him and Pittsburgh signed him to a contract. Is it any wonder where Harrison gets his drive?

Take stock of your sales team. Are they hungry? Are they focused on a higher bar, a much higher level of revenue achievement? If not, maybe it's time to stop giving participation trophies. Maybe it's time to start creating sales leaders by only rewarding winning performance.

BEING LATE IS NEVER THE SNOW'S FAULT

While watching weather reports of the record snowfall in the northeast I was reminded of why, many years ago, I was so excited to move to the warm air of Florida. I am also reminded of the sometimes uncomfortable staff conversations that accompanied bad weather.

Communities, viewers, and the general public rely on television media to get their information, especially during times of inclement weather. Many of you reading this are seated down the hall from your Doppler Radar, Klystrons or NEXRAD equipment, which your company has acquired at great expense. The meteorologists and forecasters rely upon the information generated from this equipment to inform the masses during the news, programming cut-ins or, in severe cases, wall-to-wall coverage. On a personal observation—have you noticed that the higher the rolled up sleeves the more severe the weather?

Inevitably, during snow fall social media is wrought with "what ifs" and speculation. A few of my personal favorites are, "Big project at work that I won't get to finish because of the snow" or "They cancelled school already, I hope they cancel my work" and lastly, "The snow is going to make me late for work tomorrow!"

Can you imagine if TV weather people had these excuses? Furthermore, it's NEVER the snow's fault that someone is late. Everybody knows what the weather is going to be. Certainly, safety takes priority in any situation, but my aggravation is with those who assume it's okay to set the alarm for the same time as any other day and then arrive two hours or so late, blaming the snow for their tardiness.

Anthony Stonerock had been a television AE for nearly six months when he stood in the crowd of station employees listening to my feelings about snow days. Our meteorologist was predicting a whopper of a snow storm and I wanted to remind everyone to be safe but to also plan ahead, maybe set the alarm a little earlier in anticipation of bad weather.

The next day, the community awoke to over *fifteen* inches of snowfall. So as not to have to eat my words, I arrived at the office a full 90 minutes before business hours. When I checked the sales offices I was not surprised to find Melanie Simon, our star lead-by-example General Sales Manager, already at her desk combing through inventory sheets. However, I *was* surprised to find Anthony Stonerock banging away on his computer in the sales pit. The thought that he lived 45 minutes from the office wasn't lost on me as I asked him, "What time did you leave for the office this morning?" He responded, "20 minutes ago." Doing the math, I found that hard to believe as I was guessing his bad weather home to office drive was at least 90 minutes. Sensing my confusion he continued, "I stayed at the Hampton Inn across the street so I wouldn't be late today." Wow! "Way to go Tony. I love your dedication," were the only words I could muster at that moment.

The rest of the team started rolling into the office, all with tales of the extra prep they took to be on time. One seller even had minutes to pick up warm doughnuts for the office.

But it wasn't until the end of the day, when a couple of sellers were sitting around having a bit of water cooler talk, that I realized the lesson of the day—scarcity is opportunity. While all the other reps are sleeping in and making snow excuses, the early, well-prepared seller, in absence of the competition, is able to get one-on-one, longer, more meaningful time with prospects and clients. As Anthony Stonerock commented it was like music to his ears hearing a client say, "Sure, come on over, I have time. Your competiion had to cancel because of snow."

Don't Miss Out On The Automotive Advertising Shift To Digital Products

A general sales manager told me the story of a local car dealer in his market with a $1.4 million advertising budget. The dealer spent 45%, or $630,000, of the $1.4M in online/digital advertising. How much of the dealer's digital budget did the station get? Zero.

Car dealers state the car buying cycle is now 3 months, about half of what it historically has been, and there are fewer car buyers in the sales funnel and less floor traffic from "lookers." Despite these trends, vehicle sales continue to rise. Many attribute the continued robust car sales numbers to the rise in digital advertising investments. As a result of pre-shopping via a computer screen, today's buyer steps onto a dealer's lot with knowledge of the make, model, and price of the car they're going to buy.

Does it scare you that digital is getting credit for the increase in car sales? It should, especially if you haven't incorporated steps to make sure that your sales pros are properly positioned to take advantage of the advertising shift to digital products.

You may not have the final say in what digital product investments your company is making; however, as a manager and leader you do have the ability to positively influence your team's sales success in this arena, regardless of the makeup of your digital offerings. The answer lies in four categories: people, knowledge, products, and return on investment.

People: Often when visiting television sales offices, I hear seasoned sellers reminiscing about the good old days when sales management expected sales of one thing—TV commercials. Do you have any of these nostalgic AE's on your staff? If so, the first step to digital sales success is to help these individuals understand that digital is not going away. Convergent sales are now the way of the media world and if AE's cannot get on board and get enthusiastic about selling multiple platforms, then it may be time to release them for better opportunities.

Knowledge: Too many digital sales are missed as a result of a seller's lack of knowledge about the multiple digital platforms in their sales tool box. As a sales manager, it's up to you to educate the team on the available products. Teach your AE's to listen for client needs and to recognize how the multiple platforms can be utilized to solve these needs. Spend time discussing the push and pull abilities of digital and TV and how much more powerful the results for advertisers can be when the power of digital and television are combined. To that end, make it a rule that every presentation must include digital. In today's advertising environment, I cannot think of a situation when digital inclusion is not warranted.

Products: Your office may have many offerings capable of retargeting, site optimization, reputation management, search engine marketing, etc., but mobile is the way to a car dealer's heart... and wallet.

A dealer's mobile website *should not* be a smaller version of the dealer's desktop site. Why?

Because mobile users want to connect with the dealer fast. Many times the tire kicker is standing on the lot using a dealer's mobile site to gauge unit price and selection. A mobile site that contains robust desktop-like features will slow the content load and will distract consumers. By the way, if it takes more than a thumb to navigate a mobile site, consumers will leave the site and redirect to something more navigation friendly.

Lastly, make sure to pay special attention to creatively driving leads to the dealer's *own* website. Nearly every dealer will tell you that leads to their own website are the most coveted leads. The benefit is that potential buyers on a dealer's site are looking only at the dealer's inventory vs. a third party site that provides an opportunity for consumers to compare a dealer with their competitors' inventory.

Return On Investment (ROI): Too many times a car dealer will cancel a television outlet's digital agreement because they can't attribute any sales to the effort. Third party sites like Auto Trader and Cars.com are successful because they can translate the dealer's spend into unit sales. They do this through access to dealer analytics.

To stop digital contract cancellations and build a bit of renewal insurance, train your sellers to have consistent conversations with dealer decision makers on sales expectations and return on investment models. Tie your platforms into dealer analytics to get credit for sales. If your platforms cannot do so or the dealer won't share access, then you need to determine alternative ways to measure ROI. Doing so provides tangible results and a reason for continued long-term investments in your digital offerings.

DON'T BE AFRAID TO DISCUSS PRICE

My then nearly 15-year-old daughter, Cara, walked into our living room, crying, after a babysitting job. Apparently, she had been dramatically underpaid by a neighborhood mother. Cara received only $5 for over three hours of babysitting—two toddlers! A fact she did not realize until she got inside our house and began to unfold and count the money.

As a father, I hate to see any of my kids in pain, especially in an instance that could have been avoided. However, as a sales trainer and consultant, it's extremely difficult to let moments like this pass without identifying the lesson learned.

About *two* months prior, I was proud of Cara as she canvassed our neighborhood with flyers announcing her babysitting services. However, arriving at what information Cara should include in the flyer was a sticking point between my wife, Bridget, and me. Bridget felt that surely everyone understood the going hourly rate for a babysitter and putting the per hour pay expectation on the flyer was unnecessary. I countered that it was a mistake not to define pay expectations, as at some point Cara was going to be disappointed when someone paid her short of the market rate. Can you see where this story is headed? Five dollars for three hours of work was an "I told you so" moment that I proclaimed proudly and loudly all evening.

Do you have sellers on your team who are uncomfortable discussing investment levels (price or spending on competitors) on your medium? How do your AE's respond when hit with the "how much" question? Average sellers will beat around the bush and deliver a half answer or almost apologize when stating the number. However, great sellers will, with confidence, immediately answer in some form of, "All this for only $2,740 a month (or $685 a week or just over $95 a day, etc.)." If your team is not answering the "how much" question like great sellers do, then it's up to you to prioritize more "Dealing With Price" training efforts.

How many times have you seen or heard an advertisement that touts a miracle product but doesn't list a price? These ads will often end with "call us for pricing," "click here for our best price," or "add to cart to see the price." These techniques are aggravating for the consumer and are often the root of a lost sale. Consumers guessing at a price may wrongly think that they cannot afford a product so what's the use in taking the next step to purchase? For some, the drain on personal time to jump through extra purchase hoops is a turnoff. That might explain why consumers are seeing less of these elusive price ads.

Take a look at your sales toolbox. When it comes to pricing, have you created opportunties that are advertiser friendly? Do any of your offerings come with perceived hidden agendas or are you quick to proudly disclose investment levels? Please don't misunderstand. There are advantages to showing a full presentation investment as opposed to line-by-line pricing. What I'm asking is for you to make sure your offerings are customer-focused, with investments clearly defined. And please, don't allow your sellers to assume clients understand the value of your offerings. AE's must confidently be able to explain the value of solutions assembled to solve a prospect's marketing needs.

There is a happy ending to my daughter's babysitting short pay story. That evening, while letting our dog out, I spotted what appeared to be a candy wrapper next to our driveway. To my surprise, it was actually a *twenty* dollar bill! Apparently, in the money exchange between Cara and the neighborhood mother, someone dropped the twenty. The crying stopped and celebration ensued as $5 turned into $25.

There was one more laugh that evening. Just before going to bed, we saw Cara in her pajamas in the front yard carrying a flashlight. She was looking for more dropped money!

QUESTIONS TO GAUGE THE REVENUE ATTITUDE OF YOUR TEAM

When conducting station team training I like to pose the below four questions at the start of the day to gauge the revenue attitude of the room. Feel free to use these questions at your next sales meeting. Encourage the staff to share, evaluate, and talk through their answers. Their responses may surprise you.

1) If your sales team churns $600,000 of business at the end of this year, how much revenue has to be written to make it up?

The correct answer should be north of $600,000; maybe something like $800,000 to $900,000. However, from my experience, the majority of AE's will state that they'll need $600,000 of business to offset the $600,000 loss. That kind of response is flat thinking. The key to building revenue hungry teams is to help them understand that increases are one of the major components of all forward thinking revenue conversations.

In reality, if the station is investing in capital, programming and news resources, and sales commission rates are consistent, asking for the same amount of money year to year is a loss.

2) Would each of you be happy in five years if your income is the same as it is today?

Similar to the question one explanation, personal cost of living increases indicate that a flat income is not equal to but actually less money when compared year to year.

Math aside, I would be suspect of any seller professing their satisfaction with no increase in income in a five-year window. This thinking goes against the number one motivator in commissioned sales—money.

Sellers who don't classify money in the top tier of their personal motivators are likely going to be difficult for you to keep aggressive and performing at levels required to consistently realize market audit share increases. Think of this scenario as pushing a barge upstream.

3) Can anyone honestly say that every client on your list is investing to their maximum in your digital and television spaces?

I have yet to see a seller raise his or her hand in positive response to this question. Some may respond that *many* clients are investing to their maximum but not *all* clients are doing so. This would indicate that there is room for revenue increases with existing clients.

Sellers generally make budget assumptions

without considering the entire picture. They ask a client, "What is your *TV* budget?" When the question should be, "What is your *entire marketing budget?*"

As television sales professionals we cannot hold ourselves accountable for the arbitrary reasons a prospect has assigned, say, only a hundred thousand dollars of a half million dollar marketing budget to TV. But by knowing the entire budget you could easily make a case as to why your station, cable outlet or digital products are worth more than 20% of a half million dollar budget.

Unfortunately, many reps never ask the total marketing budget question and instead are left to set their revenue ask at a percentage of the TV budget, thus, failing to maximize the client's potential investment.

4) How would your life be impacted if you were able to add another five hundred thousand or million dollars in revenue on top of your existing billing?

When you ask this question, let your team close their eyes and visualize the personal impact of this additional revenue. What could they now buy, own, support or help? Then have them visualize only half the staff delivering this increase. How transformative would that be for the entire office?

Here's the reality. Huge increases don't happen

when sellers ask for peanuts. Your folks cannot present for $500, $1,500 or $5,000 dollar increases and expect these closes to result in a half million to a million dollars in additional revenue. The asks have to be five and six digits left of the decimal point to have real, life-changing revenue impact.

Six weeks into my start as a television account executive, I was working on an advertising "package" for a prospective furniture store when the station VP & General Manager, Dave Miller, took a glance over my shoulder at the computer screen. He was less than enthusiastic about the proposal, pointing out that the store likely had over 50,000 square feet of inventory and that my one month, $1,500 ask was not nearly enough.

Dave summarized his feeling with this statement, "John, it takes just as much time and effort to prepare and ask for $10,000 for every single month of the year as it does to prepare and ask for $1,500 for one month." To this day, near the completion of every presentation, Dave's words still ring in my ears.

DON'T LET YOUR TEAM SELL LIKE DESPERATE REAL ESTATE AGENTS

When the real estate market crashed, Sarasota, Florida was one of the hardest hit geographic areas in the country. As a result, when relocating my family to Florida I was fairly confident that given the economic conditions, we were going to get a bargain on a new home. What I didn't expect to find was the glut of real estate agents selling out of fear and displaying one unprofessional move after another.

Our first example of "what not to do as a real estate agent" was Ms. One-Track Mind. Her response to everything was, "I'm expecting a near-the-asking-price offer any day, so you need to get your offer in." The problem with her statement was we had no intention of making an offer. She was trying to create demand. The agent would have been better off highlighting features and asking us a few questions. She failed to get us excited about the place or even establish our needs before attempting to close. I couldn't stop smiling when we received her desperate voicemail a week later asking us if we were still interested. Seventeen months later the house was still on the market.

Do your account executives ever do this? Do they walk in with a folder of sales packages of the month and promise advertisers big results without understanding any of the prospect's needs? Package sellers, or peddlers, are short-lived in the industry and burn out quickly. Clients want, need, and deserve customized solutions. Star managers understand and teach to this sales philosophy.

The second real estate "hot shot" I'll call Mr.

Show-Up-Late-And-Be-Dishonest. He repeatedly ignored our agent's calls. He did, however, return *my* call, probably hoping to double up on a buyer/seller commission. At the appointment, the agent was nearly a half-hour late, with no apologies. He walked us into a short-sale property where the message was crystal clear: the bank is forcing the owners to sell and the owners do not want to sell. This place had so many clothes and so much garbage strewn about that it made a college fraternity house look sterile. Standing in this mess, I burst into laughter when the agent stated, "The homeowner sincerely *does* want to sell this house."

Do you have any AE's who are consistently late for your office or team meetings? It's a pretty good bet that if they're consistently late for station meetings, they're showing up late for client meetings. At some point, their excuses become predictable and the AE loses credibility with you and with clients. Savvy clients can spot dishonesty a mile away. In the sales game, honesty is indeed the best policy.

The last example of a real estate sales agent "fail" happened with more than one agent. These agents were utilizing what I like to call "The Smothering Technique." They were determined to be at my side through every step of touring the house. Additionally, most talked so much we couldn't begin to form opinions about what we were seeing, let alone have a private conversation. Quite honestly, in these situations I just wanted to get out of the house to get away from the agent. It was pretty obvious these agents possessed the most fear and were the more desperate sellers.

There's a difference between an aggressive seller and a desperate seller. Which are you cultivating on your sales team? AE's should present confidently, ask for the close, and then go silent, waiting for the client's answer. Desperate AE's cannot stand silence and may inadvertently talk the client out of a sale.

It may interest you to know that these real estate sales gaffes are not specific to Florida. Evidence the real estate ad shocker that I saw in an Ohio newspaper, of course complete with the agent's headshot. A re-creation of the ad is provided below to protect the guilty.

FYI: SELLERS
Everybody thinks their own home is a palace. Understandably, you are emotionally attached to your home. Your Realtor will see it through more objective eyes, so don't be surprised if your house is worth less than you think.
Call me: Joe Knucklehead Realtor
(937) 555-1212

I wonder if this agent was shocked when his ad didn't get any calls?

If you ever find yourself in the market for a

new home in Sarasota, call me. I have a guy. And I guarantee he will not disappoint. Through the whole process my real estate agent was nothing short of professional and made no apologies about competing agents, despite their deficiencies. When I pushed him for comments, he simply responded, "Real Estate is not unlike any other business. Typically, the top 20% are successful. They genuinely care about their clients, are professional, and are a pleasure to deal with. The remaining 80% are just trying to make a living, and as a result, may not have the best reputations."

As I finish out this chapter, I'd like you to think about that statement. Where do your sellers fit in your market? Are they in the successful top 20% or the bottom 80%, just trying to make a living? I hope your answer is the former.

CHAPTER 4

SALES PREPARATION AND PLANNING

I believe that people make their own luck by great preparation and good strategy.

–Jack Canfield

YOU HAVE TO MAKE TIME FOR SALES TRAINING

Jim Doyle & Associates has been in the television sales training business since 1991. We often receive messages asking us to "sell up" training products to a decision maker. The requestor has recognized a training deficiency and has identified that our products or services could help with the issue. They turn to us for assistance in getting their request for purchase approved.

One of these requests arrived via email as we were prepping for a national satellite conference titled, *The Big Money Grab, Taking Lawyer Money From The Yellow Pages.* The request read: "...I would love nothing better than to listen and learn and take that Yellow Pages money and put it in MY pocket... I forwarded your information to our corporate folks asking if there was some way we could do this as a company. I was shot down. Is there any way you can convince our corporate sales management to sign on? We would be in the front of the class ready to learn!"

Did you feel the tone of rejection in this request? This guy really wants to improve. He's looking for another tool for the toolbox to enable his sales team to surpass those big budget numbers that will soon be passed down from corporate. Will this *one* satellite conference solve *all* his problems? Maybe not, but this "ask" plays into a bigger issue that could be occurring in the walls of your media outlet.

Allow me to set the stage with a hypothetical scenario, and please forgive me if it sounds vaguely familiar. You're trying to get a handle on the inventory. Political spending has created a continuous cycle of commercials coming out and going back in. AE's are not happy as their checks are smaller, while your company continues to get rich. Clients are calling. They're upset and are threatening any manager who will listen. In the middle of this pressure cooker, you're working on the upcoming budget deadline and getting ready to negotiate 1st Quarter. Don't forget to submit that corporate request on your staff's digital revenue! There's no time for AE sit-downs, no time for planning, and... no time for sales training.

Yet, when the smoke clears and the bulk of today's madness is behind you, what expectations will you lay out for your sales team? Undoubtedly, the requests of your sellers will include some form of SELLING—local direct, new business, digital, share increases, etc. Is it reasonable to expect sales to improve if there's no consistent effort for improving the skills of sellers?

Star AE's have a hunger for improvement and appreciate the value of sales teaching and training. The top 10% will make an investment in themselves by purchasing items like books and audio downloads with their own money. Great managers feed AE's with consistent, thought-provoking, skills-improving sales training. A well-trained staff is more cohesive and morale is higher. Turnover isn't a roadblock for operations that value sales training because increased performance improves incomes. Management opportunities at all levels are more plentiful as corporate begins to recognize new talent.

Back to the issue of no time for training—you have to plan for it. As a manager, you need to identify the times of the year when commitments will simply not allow you to lead or even attend some of the training sessions. When you create your annual training calendar, keeping your peak and minimal participation times in mind, be sure to spread the weekly meeting host duties among the whole sales department. Include dates for guest speakers, video sessions, field trips, and corporate training initiatives. Lastly, don't be afraid to delegate a portion of the effort to a mid-level manager or a senior AE whom you may be grooming for future management roles. Doing so will help aid your "bench building" and will relieve some of your juggling priorities stress.

OBJECTIONS AND THEIR ROLE IN NEGOTIATIONS

In a sales environment where there are sleepless nights, as we had during the "Great Recession," you can bet that your AE's faced more than their fair share of objections. In those situations, it's important to teach your sellers to understand why objections exist and how they relate to the negotiation process.

It's likely you have trained your sellers to be silent after the "ask." Any response from the client, short of "yes" or "no" is an objection. Sometimes an objection is a stall to allow the prospect to gather themselves. Sometimes a client will voice a concern. Regardless, the potential advertiser's feedback effectively "puts the ball back in your AE's court" as an invitation to negotiate. Objections are an expected part of the sales negotiation. The client is saying, "You have my interest. Tell me more."

Up to this point, the AE has delivered the "ask" and the client has responded with an objection. "Your Move" is what I like to call the next step of the discussion. This is when the AE responds to the objection moving the "ball" back to the client.

It's imperative that sellers, through their non-verbals, tone, and word structure, respond professionally and respectfully to the client's concern. Sentence openings should display empathy and start with statements like, "I understand..." or "I can appreciate what you're saying..." Disrespect, defensive postures, or an outright dismissal of the client's concern is as good as a NO SALE.

Honesty and straightforwardness trumps canned AE responses *every* time. Be sure to make a big deal of this point in your sales meeting. I suggest reviewing the Six Major Industry Objections below and combining them with additional objections unique to your market. Have your team practice responses to each of the objections until they can deliver all of them automatically and naturally. Doing so will allow your sellers to purge responses that make them uncomfortable (note that some of the responses are not for everyone) and it will aid their ability to adjust non-verbals, tones, and delivery to fit varied client personalities.

Six Major Industry Objections

1. *"Your rates are too high."*

- Compared to?
- Thank you very much. We've worked hard to get them there!
- If rate were not an issue would you be willing to invest in our station?
- If you'll allow me another minute I'd like to walk you through a Return On Investment model.
- We don't set our rates. They are purely supply and demand as determined by our advertisers.
- Yes, we're a bit higher than some of our competitors. But if you recall from the video testimonial, the reason long-standing clients say we're worth it is...

2. *"I've already spent the budget."*

- Can you help me understand how and when you allocate your budget?
- That's not a problem. Many of our clients originally had not budgeted for this. Would you be open to a return on investment review for a different perspective on how this could impact your business?
- If you were to drop one of the less than effective mediums you described earlier, would that free enough dollars to allow an

investment with me?

3. "Let me think about it."
- Can I ask, what will change between now and then?
- Do I need to go back and clarify any of the points for you?
- Sometimes when a client says *that* they're covering because they're afraid to tell me "no." Is that the case here?
- Will thinking about it make a difference in your ultimate decision?
- Are you leaning toward "yes" or "no"?

4. "You aren't the #1 station."
- You're not the #1 retailer, so I think we are perfect for each other.
- If there was only one station available to watch, you might have a point. That is not the case. There are thousands of viewers and enough to go around.
- We have discussed our station's unique ability to target your potential customers. Should we go back and review those points?
- I can find a #1 (demo/programming) story on our station if it will help ease your mind with this investment!

5. "We tried TV and it didn't work."
- I appreciate that you do not hold me

accountable for stations that may not have had your best interest at heart. However, we have 342 satisfied clients who consistently rely upon us to exceed their marketing and sales goals.

- I cannot speak to any previous experience you may have had, but do regret we didn't meet sooner so that you could have enjoyed a positive experience.
- We have been delivering customers to businesses since 1960. How could we survive if TV didn't work?

6. *"I need to discuss this with my business partner, spouse, etc."*

- Thanks for the reminder. I need to call my wife to see if she'll allow me to sell this to you!
- Let's go ahead and get this reserved with your signature. To the side of your signature, feel free to write "pending my wife's approval." That way we don't miss the production deadline.
- Perhaps we can schedule a meeting with the three of us? I promise to make you look like a hero!

BONUS! When the answer is "NO."

- Is that a "no" for today or a "no" for forever?

- I understand. Should I remove you from my contact list?
- Maybe I missed something? Can you tell me where the breakdown was so I don't make the same mistake with another client?
- I understand this is not for you. Can you think of anyone in your business circle who might get excited about this kind of partnership?

THERE'S A PAYDAY SOMEDAY

Do you ever have those moments when you hear or see something so profound that you have to capture it because you want to save it for later reflection or use?

One of those moments occurred during dinner in Dallas. I was enjoying a very passionate industry conversation with our partner station GSM, Sara Fulmer, and LSM, Mark Henager. We were nodding in agreement as each of us piled on examples of sales success and staff motivation, when Mark interjected a story that ended with one of the most insightful lines of the evening.

Growing up, Mark's dad was a minister. One of his dad's favorite quotes was from an 1880's professional baseball player turned evangelist named Billy Sunday. At this point, I stopped Mark for confirmation. "The preacher's last name was Sunday?" The thought of that struck the table as funny. Sara and I were still laughing when Mark delivered his dad's favorite Billy Sunday quote: "There's a payday someday."

Wow. I asked Mark to repeat the quote multiple times so that I could get pen to paper and capture the statement.

There's a payday someday.

Let that sink in for a moment. When used in a religious context, the dots seem easy to connect for those who believe we're held accountable for our lifetime of actions when meeting "Our Maker," and the "heaven or hell" decision is at bay.

There's a payday someday.

Being a media sales speaker and trainer, I couldn't help but think beyond religion for the statement's application. Think about your sales team(s). The work they do today will determine tomorrow's outcome. In other words, if they're prospecting, filling the sales funnel, and are efficient with their time to maximize presentation opportunities in front of decision makers, then likely, *there's a payday someday.*

The same holds true for the inverse. If a seller is poor at time management, doesn't have a formal new business prospecting plan, and lacks service skills, then they will soon find out *there's a payday someday.* Only this payday is not one that is excitedly anticipated. This payday may end with you as the manager freeing the seller for better opportunities elsewhere.

There's a payday someday.

It's what I call a pivot statement, kind of like the word *unbelievable*. As in, "Today is unbelievable." The conveyed tone relays whether the situation is good or bad.

My wish for your AE's is that when they hear, "There's a payday someday," it brings to mind positive thoughts and visions of the rewards that will soon be in hand as a result of their hard work!

IS YOUR TEAM PREPARED FOR PROGRAMMATIC BUYING?

It was a room full of sales managers and account executives. All of them sat there staring at me as though I were speaking a foreign language. It seemed that my caution to be proactive and get in front of the dramatic selling changes soon to affect our industry was falling on deaf ears. And unfortunately, this wasn't the first time.

A group VP of Sales once told me that the downfall of our business was the fax machine. Prior to the fax machine a media buyer or business decision maker would invite us to their place of business to present our sales "dance." Our competitors received the same invite. Afterward, the buyer or decision maker would reward the seller(s) with all, or a portion, of budget dollars. In those days, it wasn't necessarily the highest rated media outlet that got the bulk of the money. Instead, it was the individual who endeared him/herself to the buyer. This proved a direct correlation to the idea that buyers were buying individuals first and media outlets second.

Then, technology delivered the fax machine, followed by email. The opportunity to present the "dance" faded rapidly. The sales process consisted of little more than a few deposits around requests of, "fax/email me your avails/rates." The buyers were still able to justify shifts of dollars to their favorite sellers, but tabs, ratings, CPP's, and deliverables became larger considerations in these transactions.

Now, just around the corner in our industry, the seller is being removed altogether through a process called Programmatic buying. This new buying innovation is purely spreadsheet driven. There are no buyer/seller conversations or information exchanges in this automated trans-action system. If not you, someone in your office or company will post a percentage of your inventory to a central location that is accessible to buyers. The buyers, many who have never set foot into a cable outlet or station, let alone have ever seen a ratings book, will simply point and click on the inventory they'd like to purchase, which will be dictated by in-house data banks and preferred buy lists. There is absolutely no phone call, email or human interaction in this process.

So, what should your message be to your sales stars about Programmatic buying? The first question you should consider asking of them is, "What would happen if you came to work on Monday to find that your largest 6 or 7 accounts were gone?"

Too dramatic? I don't think so, if one considers that national accounts are the first in line for Programmatic buying, followed by regional clients and then large local clients. Any client could be drawn to the relative ease of point and click buying and your account executives will have no ability to impact the process.

Don't pull punches in this transition. Transactional sellers who are slow to change are going to be the hardest hit. Be black and white and crystal clear in your discussions about the potential negative impact Programmatic buying could have upon your sales stars' commissions.

There are too many reasons here that would indicate it's time to recondition your sellers to do the "dance." Focus your training on the power of LOCAL decision makers and LOCAL businesses and prospects. Role-play until your folks can confidently and credibly present the power of your stick and digital assets. Teach them the value of premium service after the sale. Encourage them to think in long-term partnerships instead of individual client and single month sales. Insist that they block out calendar time for prospecting and new business targeting. Hold them accountable for writing thank you's and asking for referrals. Mold your individuals into a team that has a reputation as the "go to" players in the marketplace.

Will all of this concentrated effort replace every dime that shifts to Programmatic? Maybe not in the short term. But there are many stations across the country enjoying record revenue success as a result of refocusing their local selling efforts. These stations will prove that in the long term, Programmatic buying and local selling can live in harmony in the sales office. The first step is taking the Programmatic caution seriously and enacting a plan to replace dollars that may be shifting to automated point and click Programmatic buying systems.

SEVEN TIPS TO MAKE YOUR AGENCY AVAILS STAND OUT

Star AE's understand that local direct business is key to building a solid foundation of consistent billing. However, the reality is that most AE lists consist of a blend of local direct and agency business. One of my sales manager mentors used to say, "We *covet* local direct money while *dealing* with agency buys." In conjunction with your effort to manage your team's local direct growth, it's important to provide instruction in skills needed for interaction with agencies.

Here I've listed tips to help your sales stars differentiate from the competition and better position themselves for increased agency shares. Maybe you could use these at a training meeting?

Seven Tips To Make Your Agency Avails Stand Out

1. **Never include more information than requested from the buyer.**
   - Most often, nothing more than rating and rate will suffice—no HUTS, PUTS, CPP, shares, etc.
   - Including non-requested information simply "muddies the water." Buyers don't want to have to cut through layers of info to get to the root of their request.

2. **Never send 0-rated programs.**
   - Agencies are graded on efficiencies. A zero-rated program does nothing to promote client savings.
   - Put a believable estimate on the program.

3. **Match programming to dayparts and demos.**
   - Submitting a Saturday Kids programming block on a M25-54 avail request doesn't make sense.

- Also, move all sports, specials or event programming to the top of the avail to ensure they're seen.
- Leave this type of programming in the middle of the avail and you risk losing a sales opportunity, as they may get lost in the pack.

4. **Handwrite (in blue felt-tip pen) on the avail to bring attention to specific programs.**
   - Blue ink has a calming effect. (Hey, we're looking for every edge here!)
   - Some examples of a message: "Hot show! Increased 42% book to book!" or "This show is #1 in your demo!"
   - Be sparse with your messages—only one or two every few pages.
   - I recognize that printing, writing, and then scanning as a PDF requires additional steps, but the outcome of doing so is a substantial differentiator from your competition.

5. **Make sure your station or cable logo prints on *every* avail page.**
   - Oftentimes a buyer's assistant will print out avail submissions for master grids. You are one of multiple entities submitting, which makes for a sizable stack of paper. Your logo on every page will prevent lost pages and

makes it easy on the assistant or buyer to keep track of your full submission.

- A logo on every page is simply good branding.

6. **If emailing or delivering in person, print the full avail in color.**
   - We live in a color world. Why would you ever consider black and white submissions?
   - If, for some reason, you cannot print in color, try printing the avail on a light colored pastel paper. Again, anything to stand out from the black and white competition.
   - When was the last time you hand-delivered an avail request? Chances are everyone is submitting via email. Delivering in person from time to time is another opportunity for a face-to-face buyer deposit.

7. **Write an avail rates "good until date."**
   - As an example, "Rates are good until July 6th" or "Rates are good for 10 business days."
   - This establishes a deadline and provides a bit of leverage to you, as the buyer likely assumes (rightly or wrongly) that rates may increase if the buy is not completed by a certain date.

FREQUENCY CREATES TOP OF MIND

Upon moving to Sarasota, I quickly discovered

there is only one way to get from my house to the office. It's a route that's filled with vacation condos, restaurants, sandwich and gift shops, and one 7-11 convenience store.

A couple of weeks into the daily morning drive, there was a sign posted just below the 7-11 numbers. It simply stated, "Two Glazed Donuts $1." Remember, there is only one route to get to the office, so it's safe to say that in a typical month I pass the sign nearly 40 to 50 times.

You couldn't tell it by looking at my round frame, but I am not a doughnut lover. So the simple fact that there were now cheap doughnuts near my house did nothing to motivate me to go in and make a purchase—that is, until about the 129th time I passed the "Two Glazed Donuts $1" sign.

On a late night drive from the airport after a weeklong road trip, it occurred to me that my cupboards were bare. There was no food at my house. What would I do for breakfast? At such a late hour the local grocery stores were closed and I was in no mood to drive across town to the 24-hour market. Then I remembered the 7-11 doughnuts. That night was the first time I had ever been in that particular 7-11. (The *Two Glazed Donuts for $1* actually cost $41 after recognizing that with doughnuts you need milk, bread, soda, soup, chips, etc.)

My situation is proof that frequency with a

singular message creates top of mind. When consumers are in the market for a purchase, isn't top of mind one of, if not *the,* most important marketing goal for your clients? What if the doughnut sign was up for only one day? Would it have the same impact? Not likely. Unless the message is extremely creative, bad or high profile, who remembers advertisements they have seen only once? It took me 129 times of seeing that advertisement before I was in the market to purchase. But when it came time to make the decision, that message was the first and only impression that crossed my mind. As a result, 7-11 got my business.

Since then, how many times have I been back to the 7-11? Four. I guess I was wrong about not being a doughnut lover.

LEAVE VOICEMAILS THAT GET RETURNED

Have you ever been on the receiving end of a voice message from a less than professional salesperson and not hung up? Because we're a company of sales trainers, I often listen to voicemails in their entirety, despite the overwhelming urge to delete most of the ramblings before the twenty-second mark.

One of the most memorable messages was a two-minute and twenty-six second voicemail from a software rep. Here are a few observations resulting from that call: 1) when it comes to voicemails, less is more; 2) the caller had no clue *or* care of my needs, and proceeded to pitch in the message; and 3) because of this experience, this software company will never get business from me.

Below are a few suggestions to make sure your account executives *don't* sound like unprofessional peddlers, and to help increase the number of calls returned.

1. **Write a script for voice-mail messages**. Too many times AE's launch into random talk when the "beep" sounds. A voice-mail "road map" will ensure the AE stays on task and gets the major points into the message.

2. **Get to the point** because the prospect's finger is on the delete button. If the "hook" isn't in the first few seconds of the message, it's likely to get deleted before completed.

3. **Ideally a message should be 30 seconds or less**. Don't allow your sales team to give the sales pitch in a message. The goal is to get a return call, in order to get an appointment.

4. **Give the recipient a compelling reason to return the call**. For example, when calling an attorney the message might say, "Mr. Legal, I have an idea that is helping lawyers across the country increase both

the number and quality of cases. But timing is crucial, as this idea can only be shared with a few select attorneys."

5. To minimize "phone tag," **detail the best times to return the message**. "You can reach me between 3 and 5 today or 7 and 10 tomorrow."

6. **A smile can be heard without being seen**. Smiling adds enthusiasm and positive inflection to a voice. As a sales manager, I purchased small mirrors to hang in each AE's cubicle to remind them to smile.

7. **Speak clearly, confidently and with purpose**. People like doing business with winners. Sound like a winner.

8. **End each message by giving your telephone number** at a pace in which it can be written down—*twice*. Don't forget a "thank you."

Back to the voicemail from the software rep. I'm still trying to determine if the end request in this call was gutsy or just plain sales stupidity. The message closed with, "...Robert (yes, called me by the wrong name), if you are not the person responsible for the software purchases in your company, call me back as I need to know the name of the person that is responsible for software purchasing." Click...

I'm guessing this rep was not the salesperson

of the month!

A SALES MEETING FOR OBJECTIONS

Earlier in this chapter, I wrote of *Objections and Their Role In Negotiations.* This is a topic that needs repetition and should be on your sales training calendar multiple times throughout the course of the year. One of the most opportune times for refresher training on handling advertiser objections is when your sales stars are building their client call lists and preparing for their annual diagnosis and renewal meetings.

The key to hosting a sales meeting on objections is to list every anticipated "road block" that clients may throw at your AE's. Then, as a staff, you should work through the list line by line until each member of your team is confident in their response. Make it a game and award prizes for the best answers. It's likely there will be multiple answers to each objection. That's the bonus from this exercise. The multiple answers allow each of your sellers to choose which response is most comfortable for their individual sales style. Don't be afraid to repeat this meeting a couple of times a year. In this category of training, practice does indeed make perfect.

In addition to the Six Major Industry Objections outlined previously, below are a few objections to help you get started. Think of additions you might add to the list to challenge your sellers at your next sales meeting.

Objections

- We already have a plan in place with WPDF and I don't feel like your presentation is reason enough to change our plans.
- Right now my boss will not authorize more money for the advertising budget.
- Your rates are too high.
- My customers don't use the web to find my product.
- I need to think this over. Can you call me in a month?
- I've never had good results with TV/Radio/ Cable.
- I don't want to stick my neck out on this. If it fails, I'll be left answering to the owner.
- How do you know it will work?
- I'm still not sure how many people have heard of your station.
- I tried your cable a while back and wasn't happy with the results.
- I've been doing business with the other guys for over fifteen years and it seems to work just fine.
- When I did TV the last time I didn't see my commercials.
- I want to cancel my TV commercials and

just use digital.
- I just don't know if I should buy from you.
- KHCM is a lot less per commercial and they give me a lot of added value in their news.
- I'm in an annual contract with ____ and am not sure I can get out of it.
- We can't afford it.
- I don't click on any of the ads and I'm pretty sure nobody else does.
- That has value, just not for me.
- We've cut way down on our spending because of lack of sales.
- You need to give me a guarantee this will work.
- I'm happy with Google AdWords.
- Your cost per points are way out of line compared to the market.
- Your station isn't #1.
- I like the creative idea, but I'm not comfortable with being tied to your noon news. Does anyone watch it?
- I can get these commercials cheaper somewhere else. Do you want to sharpen your pencil and come back?
- We're happy with what we're currently doing.
- We just use digital. I don't need TV commercials.

- After we spoke last time, I started looking and I don't see any other doctors in my field using TV. I think commercials would make me look desperate.
- We haven't advertised on TV, cable or radio for two months and sales have not gone down at all.
- The market is severely down for our entire industry. We're leaning toward a more direct, affordable way to reach customers without wasting a lot of marketing dollars. TV isn't part of that mix right now.
- I want to be on the good shows like *Dancing With The Stars, Survivor,* and *NCIS.* I don't watch your shows.
- Can you really get people into my store with commercials airing in repeats on your station?
- I'm not interested.

LIVE BY THE RATINGS, DIE BY THE RATINGS

On the way to an appointment in a cross town car ride, a junior AE voiced her concern over a competitor's recent ratings surge. The question was, "How can we compete with CBS's 3.7 rating when we only have a 2.1 rating?" My answer was, "Don't sell ratings—take them (ratings) out of the negotiation."

My first TV sales manager, Dale Woods, used to

say, "Live by the ratings, die by the ratings." His point was that ratings victories can be short-lived. Further, a media outlet that's number *one* today could easily finish number *four* in the next sweeps. Viewing increases can certainly be a part of the conversation, but in conversations with local decision makers, the foundation of the sales pitch should *not* rest on ratings performance alone.

In any market, USA, average talent media managers encourage sales teams to blanket the market with *any* ratings story that trumps a competitor. Somewhere, right now, a client is sitting patiently and listening as a rep proudly proclaims, "We're number one with 13 year olds at 2am on Tuesdays!" How embarrassing for the rep and for our business!

If you're one of our UPGRADE Selling® partners, you're familiar with our Jim Doyle & Associates presentation template. The summary reflects a few category and investment totals, but an individual program's rating and rate are never discussed. The majority of the presentation is spent elaborating on the client's Unique Selling Proposition (USP) and how we intend to creatively convey that differentiator. In effect, we are selling the idea. In these presentations, the client has *never* asked me, "I see you've included morning news. What kind of rating does that show get?" How is this possible? It's because the "idea" sells the proposal. As a result, individual show ratings and rates are an after-thought.

Make it a point in your next sales meeting to condition your sales stars to get potential advertisers excited about ideas that will help them move more products for the client. Doing so will differentiate your team from the market competitors, who will be left to fight with clients over impressions, clicks, cost per point, cost per thousand, and cost per spot.

PEOPLE DO BUSINESS WITH PEOPLE THAT THEY KNOW, LIKE, AND TRUST

My friend Dan Marchese retired from TV sales years ago. I had the great pleasure of working with him at two different companies, as both of our careers required multiple titles and time zones.

The one thing that always amazed me with Dan was his ability to instantly connect with clients. Whether a current advertiser or prospect, they always seemed to have time to speak with their "friend." So it wasn't a surprise to hear, despite being more than four years removed from his last TV sales job, that on a fairly regular basis he still reaches out to and hears from his ex-clients.

Dan shared an email from one of those ex-clients with me and he wanted to know, "Are the new crop of TV sellers really that bad? Do they not understand the value of building relationships?"

The email (with names changed to protect the guilty) reads:

Dan,

What a pleasure to hear from you. We are still at it. I am sorry that you left. Between you and I, it upsets me that Sharon was handed our account. She is not worthy of our business. You are the one that cultivated my account and your persistence paid off. Many media salespeople come in but none of them get it the way that you did. You spent the time to come by once in a while even when I was not buying and you took the time to build a relationship. These new guys do not understand that if they don't get me to sign on the first time they throw down a deal they never come back. You on the other hand were smart enough to know that people do business with people that they know, like, and trust. Sharon only fits one of those, where as you fit all 3. If you have any suggestions for me, please let me know.

Thanks for dropping me a line. I hope that you are in good health and enjoying whatever you are doing.

Best wishes to you!

Barry

Can you sense the frustration from the client? He feels the seller was "handed" the account. It's as though the advertiser is a dollar sign. He gets attention when he's spending money and doesn't hear from the rep when the money isn't being spent. The rep isn't making deposits and the client feels shorted.

How many clients would be candid enough to share these thoughts with the new rep? Likely, not many. Instead, the lack of relationship continues to build resentment and the advertiser's perceived investment begins to feel like a "spend." At that point, it's convenient for the client to move their money to another outlet that will take the time to understand his business needs. Then the account moves into the non-returning category or it's moved to another new AE and the relationship process, or lack thereof, with the client starts all over again.

This topic is worth discussion in your sales meeting. To amplify the lesson—*without* revealing the questions before the meeting—ask things about their key accounts like:

- Do you know how many kids the decision maker has? Boys or girls? Their ages?
- Where does the business owner like to vacation?
- Are they sports fans? What sports and team?
- Married? How long? How many times?
- Did they attend college? Where?

- What would they be doing if they didn't own X business?
- What did they do before this business?
- What kind of car do they drive? Why?
- Do they have a favorite meal?
- What's their favorite color?
- Dog or cat?

If you read the list of questions in one sitting it comes off as intrusive or a nosey interview. However, these and similar topics come naturally as relationships grow. The answers from your AE's will provide a gauge on the depth of their connection with the account. Ultimately, if there is no connection, there'll be a time when there is no account.

As Dan's ex-client expressed, "People do business with people that they know, like, and trust." It's that simple.

A HOT PROSPECTING CATEGORY THAT'S ONLY GETTING HOTTER

Not too many years ago, there was a class of attorneys who frowned at the notion of advertising their profession. They believed that marketing oneself somehow cheapened the perception of the established legal institution. Thankfully, to the benefit of sales and marketing professionals, solo practitioners to mega-firms now generally accept the notion of advertising. In many instances, the *acceptance* has progressed to a *need* for marketing legal offerings.

The Bureau of Labor Statistics (www.bls.gov), projects that by 2024, the number of attorneys in the United States will have grown 6%. The news gets better, as in a typical year 58 million consumers in the U.S. sought help from one of the over 1.2 million licensed attorneys in the U.S. and 76 percent of consumers used the Internet to search for an attorney.*

By the way, 26 percent of lawyers end up in private practice, which is the prospecting "sweet spot" for your local direct sales stars.

The Bureau of Labor Statistics continues the good news for television advertising by predicting that wider availability and affordability of legal clinics will result in an increased use of legal services for middle-income consumers. Bingo! Your legal prospect has a need and you have the ultimate medium to creatively position and differentiate the attorney from the legal masses competing for these consumers.

When was the last time you called or stopped by a lawyer's office to discuss what they could do for you in case you were ever in a car accident or decided to file bankruptcy or get divorced? The answer is probably never. However, it's a pretty good bet that you've visited a furniture store or car dealer "just looking," long before you were in the market to purchase.

Attorneys are *similar* to other advertising categories in that they need to establish top of mind awareness. They *differ* from other advertisers because they are unable to create special promotions to drive traffic to attract tire kickers. The legal business is a need-based business. Consumers don't call attorneys until after the accident has happened. As a result, it's even more important for your legal clients to push frequency, own dayparts, and have a crystal clear memorable and differentiating message. (*https://en.wikipedia.org/wiki/Attorneys_in_the_U nited_States)

BE "PATIENT" WITH HEALTH CARE

Many doctors will readily admit that medical school did not provide them with the business skills to know how to negotiate with insurance companies, manage an office staff or execute a marketing plan. Add to the mix uncertainty about legislation and competition for newly insured patients and one can understand why docs are beginning to explore advertising options. Now, more than ever, healthcare professionals are prepared to listen to your marketing professionals and are curious about the delivery power of your programming and digital products.

I was shocked when a Southeastern surgeon

explained that for a simple routine surgery, after hospital billing, anesthesiology fees, miscellaneous charges and insurance calculations, she receives about 3.5% of the total bill. So, on a $20,000 billable hospital surgery her office claims about $700.

In West Virginia, a family doctor expressed concern that more than 85% of his patients are on Medicaid and Medicare insurance. "Pretty tough to make a living when you're only getting a 40% reimbursement rate," the doctor mumbled.

Please don't misunderstand. I'm not suggesting we break out the tissues in pity over the kind of money doctors are *not* getting. I'm simply making the point that the money no longer automatically flows just because someone has completed medical school.

In response to income declines and general unhappiness with hospital contracts, the solution for many surgeons is to combine forces and open care, surgery or specialty centers outside the oversight of hospitals. In these new environments, surgeons are no longer obligated to financially suffer under rising hospital fees, and because of this, the overall bill to patients is lower. The bonus for these docs is that their fees are higher—in many instances three to four times as much as the hospitals are paying. As a result, they perform fewer surgeries and can spend more individual time with patients, all while making more money. But to be successful, the market has to be aware of these new centers. The move from contracted security to starting a new venture is an entrepreneurial risk that not all in the medical community are equipped to, or want to, pursue. The alternative for docs reluctant to hang a business shingle is to accept hours and pay ceilings that accompany many hospital or group service contracts.

Many family docs, with a rising number of low reimbursement insurance patients, are finding some financial relief by getting qualified in procedures that are not covered by insurance. These docs go for an extended weekend to become certified to administer botox, restylane or disport. Some are investing in machines to conduct procedures like Coolsculpting, Liposonix, Cellulaze or Strawberry Laser. Regardless of the certification or procedure, the "cash" opportunity can offset a portion of the insurance losses—assuming the public knows about the additions to the practice.

A funny thing happens if one throws a party and doesn't send invitations—no one shows! That's the same logic that applies to these medical centers and practice additions. If the community is unaware of the changes then how will they know to call these doctors? That's why your sellers are in an incredible position. These medical professionals are looking for solutions to their advertising needs or, at a minimum, clarity, on a marketing plan.

As you encourage your team to prospect health care, some AE's may try to beg off the category by claiming all the big hospitals are controlled by agencies. This push for medical has nothing to do with hospitals and should not stop at targeting surgery centers or new family practice additions. Your team needs to think way outside hospital marketing. For example, not long ago I saw a TV commercial for a gastrointestinal center and several years ago, in Memphis, Tennessee, there were *three* limb replacement centers running commercials in the market!

Finally, a warning. The healthcare sales cycle is typically much longer when compared to other advertising categories. But don't let your sellers be so quick to give up, because the average dollar close is infinitely higher. A little persistence and a dedication to closing something, even small agreements with each call (for example, the next appointment, a creative idea or programming plan), will go a long way toward posting huge revenue wins for your sales stars.

A SALES MEETING OF THANKS

Many years ago, my wife Bridget gave me an article that was being circulated as the philosophy of

Charles Schulz, the creator of the Peanuts comic strip. Since then, I have discovered that this "philosophy" first appeared in the book, *G.R.A.C.E: The Essence Of Spirituality,* written by pastor Dennis Fakes.

In the spirit of thanks, maybe you could share it with your team at the end of one of your sales meetings?

A Reminder Of Who Is Important In Your Life

You don't actually have to answer all of the below questions. Just reflect on them.

- Name the *five* wealthiest people in the world.
- Name the last *five* Heisman trophy winners.
- Name the last *five* winners of the Miss America contest.
- Name *ten* people who have won the Nobel or Pulitzer Prize.
- Name the last half dozen Academy Award winners for best actor and actress.
- Name the last decade's worth of World Series winners.

How did you do? Not so stellar? The point is, none of us remember the headliners of yesterday. There are no second-rate achievers. They're the best in their fields. But the applause dies. Awards tarnish. Achievements are forgotten. Accolades and certificates are buried with their owners.

Here's another quiz. See how you do on this one:

- List a few teachers who aided your journey through school.
- Name *three* friends who have helped you through a difficult time.
- Name *five* people who have taught you something worthwhile.
- Think of a few people who have made you feel appreciated and special.
- Think of *five* people you enjoy spending time with.
- Name a half dozen heroes whose stories have inspired you.

Easier? Probably. The lesson: people who make a difference in your life are not the ones with the most credentials, the most money or the most awards. They are the ones who care.

Sometimes the rush of business may result in us taking some relationships for granted. We may, unknowingly, overlook the assistance of a few who helped to make our individual success possible. Please make it a point to show appreciation to the individuals who have made, or continue to make, a difference in your life.

CHAPTER 5

WITHOUT CUSTOMERS YOU HAVE NO BUSINESS

If you work just for money, you'll never make it, but if you love what you're doing and you always put the customer first, success will be yours. -Ray Kroc

A CUSTOMER SERVICE LESSON FROM DELTA PILOTS

Have you noticed a trend on Delta Airlines? They're really working hard to upgrade their customer "touch," and it goes way beyond a smiling "thank you for flying..." as you exit the plane. Now, *pilots* are walking the aisles pre-flight, telling stories, asking questions, cracking a few jokes, and in general, making a memory by upgrading the flier experience in a competitive category.

When telling this story, many times the

feedback I receive is some form of, "The pilot? The one flying the plane comes out and greets people?" For many, it's hard to believe that someone so important would take the time to interact with a customer.

It's the same in our business. Sometimes the bigger the title, the less time one spends talking to clients. Perhaps the client senses an air of, "The one who runs the media outlet is too 'important' to spend any time with the likes of me." I'm confident that's not the message you want to send.

When going on calls with general managers, I love to ask a client, "When was the last time you saw the general manager from one of our competitors?" The overwhelming response is some form of, "Never."

Look, I know you have a ton of responsibility and that many times internal or corporate issues get in the way of well-intended efforts to go on calls with AE's, but these instances should be the exception, not the norm. This topic brings to mind the AE who stopped asking the GM to go make a deposit with a client. "I've told the client I was bringing the 'Big Boss' to see them," she said to me, "but then I'd show up without him and you could see the disappointment in the client's eyes."

As the leader of the organization, you need to prioritize and make time to see the clients who have confidence in and support your team with their hard-earned dollars. It's as simple as setting aside time for a weekly thank you lunch, or a list of client thank you voicemails after hours, or a thank you letter. Once you comfortably accomplish those baby steps, then it's time to step into a larger prioritized commitment—actually setting aside at least a half-day a week to go on calls with AE's. If you want to have fun with the exercise, randomly draw from AE business cards at a sales meeting to determine which sales star gets the pleasure of your company during their sales appointments that day.

The worst first time to meet a client is when there's a problem. Beat them to the punch with an effort to say "hello" and show appreciation, long before any problems surface. Later, when there's a speed bump in the relationship, thanks to something like a traffic code or copy issue, the communication will be much more cordial because the client has already met the "big title" and they appreciate their status as an important customer.

WHAT CLIENTS LOVE

In the process of moving from Dayton, Ohio to Sarasota, Florida, I dreaded the prospect of combing through "junk" and filling boxes that only got dumped and restacked at the new destination. However, for those of you who have endured a move, you'll relate when I tell you I found an upside to packing. Sometimes you find a "gem" that you'd forgotten you even owned. One such "gem" for me was a book by sales and marketing consultant and best-selling author, Harry Beckwith called, *What Clients Love, A Field Guide To Growing Your Business.* It was published in 2003 and the tattered pages reminded me of its use during many sales meetings.

One of my favorite sections in the book is called "Nine Rules of Business Manners." We used to encourage AE's to print them out and hang them prominently in their cubicles. The instructions read: put a copy where you can see it and re-read these regularly. Living by these rules will make your business and life—yours and others—richer in every sense of the word.

Nine Rules of Business Manners

1. Always wait a split second after a person finishes talking before you speak.
2. Listen with your entire body.
3. Be positive.
4. Speak well of others.
5. Memorize names.
6. Never try to impress. The effort always shows and it diminishes you.
7. Never make your conversations—particularly on cell phones—public.
8. Praise but never flatter. Praise makes

people feel good; flattery makes them feel manipulated.

9. A simple rule whenever you're in doubt: be kind.

The book ends by making the point that passion and belief in yourself is your greatest asset. Clients love that.

What Clients Love is worth the read. Maybe you can find a copy in one of your moving boxes?

THREE MANAGEMENT "MUST DO" SOFT DEPOSITS

Can you think of a time when your first introduction or conversation with a client was when they had an issue with your organization? When the client is demanding a "general to general" meeting or appointment because an AE doesn't have the guts or authority to solve the client's issue? Without ever having reached out to the client previously, you're an unknown and these meetings, for you, can be defensive, judgmental, and frustrating.

How different are these meetings if you have previously acknowledged a client? Sure, there could still be some uncomfortable moments, but in general, these encounters tend to be a bit smoother since the client at least has a working knowledge of you based upon your previous communication.

The reality is that most managers are hard-pressed to know *every* client who does business with their station or cable outlet. Today, I'm suggesting *three* management "must do" soft deposits that will leave *every* client with a great feeling about you and will portray you as one who is grateful and committed to service. That's not a bad reputation to have when the client contacts you for help with an issue.

1. New Business Thank You

At the end of each month, *all* new, first-time-on-your-air or digital advertisers should receive a thank you letter via US mail signed by the GM, GSM, and AE. Doing so reflects full team support.

In the case of a new agency account, a letter should go to the agency and to the owner or decision maker of the business for which the agency is placing the buy. (Hey, they're your client as much as they are the agency's client!)

The letter should be on your branded letterhead and should include business cards. Here's a sample:

Dear Mark,

Congratulations on your decision to partner with NBC 7 television! Your trust and confidence in our station, your AE Jason, and the rest of our NBC 7 team is absolutely appreciated. Our goal is to provide you with continued impeccable service and a record return on your investment.

We're looking forward to a long and mutually beneficial relationship and encourage you to contact us at any time for assistance.

Thank you for your investment and partnership!

Jim Wilson, Vice President & GM
Sharon Hess, General Sales Manager
Jason Watson, Account Executive

2. Management Phone Message

This deposit technique always receives rave reviews from the recipient. The key is to call outside of business hours to be able to leave a detailed and sincere thank you for the client's business.

- Each Friday, the sales team should provide a few names and phone numbers (no mobile phones) of advertisers they would like a manager to call. Again, these names are for thank you deposits, not to cover problems or issues.
- The GM and GSM split up the list (usually not more than 3 or 4 names each) and leave a voicemail in the spirit of the below:

"Hi Bruce.

This is John Hannon, General Manager of WQAE and I'm phoning you this morning to say thank you. Sometimes we get so caught up in the rush of business we forget to say thank you loudly enough. We understand that our success is only possible because of the investment you continue to make in our station. Thank you, Bruce. Should you ever need to reach me, my name again is John Hannon. I am the General Manager of WQAE and my direct line is 937-776-4997; that's 937-776-4997. We absolutely appreciate your partnership, Bruce."

I used to leave these messages on the way to my kids' Saturday morning sports games or on the way to/from Sunday mass. These were great general to general deposits to help jump-start a client's Monday morning.

3. End Of The Year Thank You Letter

The holiday season is a perfect time to show client appreciation, and is an even better opportunity to deliver a "general to general thank you" deposit. *Every* client who invested their hard-earned dollars with your TV station or cable outlet, regardless of the size of the order or where (programming, digital, production, etc.), should receive a thank you letter from either the general manager or sales manager or both, with a business card(s).

Below is an example of an end of the year thank you letter that should be mailed before the start of the New Year.

Dear Jan,

Too often in the rush of business life we fail to say "thank you" loudly enough. As 2015 becomes a memory, I want to extend my sincere appreciation to you for your business, partnership, and confidence in our television station. It is only through your support that NBC 25 was able to establish yet another record year!

We're looking forward to the challenges of 2016, and encourage you to continue to rely upon us for assistance in exceeding your marketing goals.

Sincerely,

Jim Winger, VP & General Manager, NBC 25 Television
Cheri Carlson Director of Sales, NBC 25 Television

Please note that the letter is cosigned by both the GM and DOS. Feel like adding a bit more appreciation? Add signature lines from the LSM, Digital Manager, Research Director, Production Manager, or any title that would have the opportunity to interact with the client. The key is to show genuine appreciation from the top manager and the team. Doing so will differentiate you from the well-meaning competitors in your market who never seem to have the time to get around to making these kinds of deposits.

For those long-time loyal accounts, here's a final idea to kick your deposit up a notch. Below the signature lines, handwrite a post script with a tangible extra, something like, "Please note the addition of bonus commercials on your December invoice. These are a thank you for your loyalty to our station. Merry Christmas!"

Notice that the message doesn't tie you down as to how many or where the commercials will be placed. Even without that information, the deposit still has the service effect of appreciation and sincerity in advancing the client's business.

For those of you reading who are always looking for the extra edge (and who isn't?), remember to always sign your signature and any postscripts or written messages in blue. Why? Because research has shown that blue is a calming color and readers are more receptive and at ease with blue ink vs. a color like black.

YOU HAVE THE POWER TO MAKE TODAY A GREAT DAY

It was 6:50am on a Saturday morning. Ten minutes prior I tipped an airport restaurant waitress twenty bucks on a $7 breakfast tab. Why? Because the waitress took special care to serve up an early morning helping of smiles to make sure that not only I, but all diners, enjoyed a positive start to a long day of travel. On any other day her effort may have gone unnoticed by me, but today, I've made a conscious decision to be on the lookout for opportunities to make it a great day. Wait, I'm getting ahead of the story...

The last 24 hours had been a traveler's nightmare. The day before, an early arrival at a small *eight*-gate airport turned into multiple delays, missed connections, and 117 disgruntled passengers, not hiding their disgust of Delta gate agents. It always amazes me the number of individuals who loudly unload their displeasure on airline gate agents, the only individuals responsible for making the final decision on who goes or stays behind when the plane fires its engines. Ultimately, the agent was able to get me to Atlanta the same night, but unfortunately, long after the last flight from Atlanta to Sarasota had flown. As a result, I was re-booked on an early morning flight and had to stay in an Atlanta hotel on Delta's dime.

The strain of a productive but long work week and uncontrollable travel frustration, which was now cutting into weekend family time, must have been written all over my face. The hotel's airport shuttle driver stood next to me in the early morning dark. With a great big grin he said, "Bet you're anxious to get home." In frustration, I'm thinking this guy is the master of the obvious. He continued, "Look at that beautiful sun coming up over there. Seeing it never gets old. It's like the sun wakes up smiling every day, like it's telling me, 'make it a great day.'"

Whoa! Some people pay as much as $150 an hour for this kind of couch session, but this shuttle driver was passing out mental fixes for free!

Call it spiritual guidance, karma, right-place-right-time, whatever, this shuttle driver was spot-on with his observation and created within me an immediate state-of-mind shift.

When the sun rises it marks the start of something new. It's kind of nature's "do-over." We can choose to put the previous day's hassles behind us, learn from the experiences, and make today a better and more productive opportunity or we can accept the alternative, continuing to live in the moments of the past and allowing negative baggage to weigh us down. Until meeting the shuttle driver it had never really occurred to me how much power we possess in making a day good or bad, not just for ourselves but for everyone we encounter.

I wasted no time extending the driver's grin to other passengers, helping with their bags and holding doors open. The return "thanks" and positive greetings were instant energy. Once inside the airport, my smiles and generosity continued by allowing those in a rush to move ahead and making small talk with passengers and TSA agents.

As a manager, many times you are on the receiving end of bad news. How often do you reveal your negative baggage? What kind of feedback do you receive in those instances? Resistance? Avoidance? Negativity? Try putting on a positive air. Compliment new ties and blouses. Praise great work. Ask, and genuinely get excited about, an employee's family. Display an "attitude of gratitude" and watch as the day begins to snowball with positive momentum.

Sitting at the airport restaurant, realizing that the waitress had made a conscious decision to have a positive impact on everyone's day, I wondered if she had ever met the airport shuttle driver. I was glad I had met him.

A SALES LESSON FROM A SERVER NAMED MICHAEL

By now you have likely determined that I spend a lot of time on the road. Because Atlanta is the Delta hub that connects all flights to and from my Sarasota, Florida home, I've come to know the airport quite well. Whenever time allows, I stop to eat at the T.G.I. Friday's in Atlanta's Terminal B. Why? It's *not* the taste of the food. There are tastier airport options. I go there to eat and enjoy the service of a waiter named Michael.

What makes him so special? He looks you in the eye and engages you the moment you're seated. He confidently and sincerely offers, "Thank you for choosing to dine at T.G.I. Friday's. I am Michael and it is my pleasure to serve you."

Early in our careers we're taught that one never gets a second chance to make a first impression. How would clients describe their first meeting with your sales stars? Is the meeting memorable, in a positive way?

If choosing a meal becomes a difficult decision, Michael is armed with menu suggestions that are "prepared especially for you." Not once have I doubted my menu pick. Why? Because Michael supports my decision. He delivers an enthusiastic "Congratulations on an excellent choice," followed by, "You are really going to enjoy that selection."

Writing this, I'm reminded of once observing an account executive and sales manager close a $28,000 agreement. Would you believe that after the client signed they didn't thank him for the business? Not once! Thinking about it, that's not the only time I have witnessed a lack of appreciation after a client signed a contract. The waiter at Friday's is working for a $12 check and maybe a $4 dessert upsell and I lost track of the multiple thank you's offered during the meal.

Are your sellers expressing their true appreciation for the business that clients entrust to them? Sure, we all have bad days, but to express a less than enthusiastic response over a business owner's marketing investment is unacceptable.

Michael isn't perfect. Sometimes he does make a mistake. In one instance, the soup I ordered never arrived. The entrée hit the table without a mention of soup. I hesitated to tell Michael, knowing he would not take the news lightly. His response was predictable in that he took full responsibility, made no excuses, apologized profusely, and wanted to know how he could fix the mistake.

At Jim Doyle & Associates we believe, "You should treat your stars differently." If someone is a workhorse, a consistent performer, a star, they are likely harder on themselves than you could ever be on them. It makes no sense to ride them on trivial items. Instead, get out of their way and let them do what they do best—sell and serve clients and customers.

The way the bill is presented is another of Michael's differentiators. When bringing the check to the table he states, "I'm here when you need me." With that simple statement Michael is conveying his respect for a customer's time. In other words, stay if you have time or go if you have a plane to catch. Regardless, he will pick up your payment when *you* are ready.

The icing on the cake (pun intended) is when he brings you the change. Michael looks you in the eye and states, "I appreciate you."

Not once does this server ever give me a chance to feel my business is taken for granted. His customer service and care are impeccable *and* sincere. As a result, it's likely that Michael gets considerably higher tips than the other servers, and he should—he deserves it.

Would it be safe to say that if your sales team displayed similar traits they would enjoy larger, more consistent revenue wins? The answer is a resounding "yes." In media sales, as it is in the restaurant business, the win is in the compounding of renewals and repeat business and that's when the big money strikes.

If I'd not had the pleasure of being served by Michael, it's a good bet that I would *not* have gone back to T.G.I. Friday's in the airport. But now, because of a waiter who refuses to settle for average, I will take every opportunity to go back to that restaurant.

Stop by the T.G.I. Friday's in Terminal B on your next trip through the Atlanta airport and ask to be served by Michael. Don't be surprised if you see me there!

IGNORING A CUSTOMER'S COMPLAINT IS A HUGE MISTAKE

While standing in the National car rental line, I couldn't believe my ears. A competing rental car company, Alamo, was within earshot of National's counter. The conversation between the Alamo rep and a customer was as follows:

Customer: *I rented a car from you 2 days ago. A couple of hours ago, I noticed the car was leaking a lot of oil and making a funny noise. I left my family at the beach and immediately drove the car back here to exchange it. One of your lot guys is looking at the car now.*

Alamo rep: *How many miles did you drive the car?*

Customer: *I'm not sure. We've been taking in the local sights and going from the condo to the beach. It has been in-town driving.*

Alamo rep: *Did you return the car with a full tank of gas?*

Customer (now getting a little heated): *The car sounds like it's a block from breaking down and you want me to stop for gas?!*

Alamo rep: *You signed a contract stating that when you returned the car it would have a full tank of gas. There will be a charge to you for the cost of filling up the vehicle...*

At this point, the customer turns three shades of red and unloads on the rental car rep with words that are not fit for this writing.

What just happened here? I'm guessing Alamo just lost a customer for life.

The rental company's car was faulty. There

are so many things the rep could have done to massage the inconvenience the customer was experiencing. The first step should have been a sincere apology and a reassurance that the problem will quickly get fixed. Maybe an upgrade car could have been offered. Unfortunately, the rep did neither and instead chose to focus on collecting gas money.

When one of your clients is upset over a legitimate AE mistake, how do your sellers handle the situation? My hope is that they apologize, take the complaint seriously, and then immediately go about fixing the wrong and trying to win back the client's trust.

If the situation is something the AE cannot handle, they will likely come to you for help. Your role is to set the example for your sales pro by immediately calling the client to smooth over the situation. Clients will appreciate contact from a manager who's taking responsibility and is re-confirming the importance of the relationship. If handled correctly, many times this call can turn a mistake into a giant win for the company.

As a case in point, during my second year as an AE, our traffic department scheduled Memorial Day copy for a furniture store's July 4th weekend sale. The first thing on Monday morning, the furniture store owner called to unload her disappointment on me.

I immediately got the LSM involved, who called the owner to apologize. As soon as the LSM finished the call, we hopped into his car, picked up two dozen doughnuts, and drove to the furniture store. We walked straight to the owner's office and delivered the doughnuts and a card with this written message: *Mistakes happen, but that's no excuse for running the wrong copy for your weekend sale. There will be no charge for the "wrong copy" commercials. In addition, we will add a bonus, matching schedule to your next weekend sale. We absolutely appreciate and value your business and apologize to you and your staff for the inconvenience.*

At the end of the week, the client added money to her commercial schedule—proof that our sincere apology worked and that she was able to move forward with our relationship as though the mistake had never happened.

WAITING AT THE DOCTOR'S OFFICE

Have you ever burned daylight sitting at the doctor's office waiting to be seen? How long do you wait? I'll typically wait about 15-20 minutes before making my way back up to the check-in window with an exasperated, "Is the doctor going to be much longer?" question.

If you've been in this situation, you have likely mumbled, "Yeah right," after the receptionist smiles, apologizes, and tells you the wait is just a few more minutes. In the sales game, time is money. So once the wait approaches a half-hour, my patience wears thin and I will typically ask for a reschedule and then leave.

That's pretty much the scenario I was faced with, when at about the 20-minute mark I got the obligatory "just a few more minutes" line from the receptionist. However, somewhere around the 35-minute mark, something happened that absolutely took me by surprise and erased any thoughts of an exit.

The doctor approached me in the waiting room, extended a hand to greet me, and said, "Mr. Hannon, we had a bit of an emergency, which has created back log this morning. I apologize for your wait. If you allow us just a few more minutes, I'll see you as soon as I dismiss the next patient." She continued, "Would you like a water or soda while you wait? Again, thank you for your patience."

Can we pause right here and digest what just happened? Because of this doctor's quick check-in, I went from *frustrated and ready to walk out the door* to *holy cow raving fan*.

Do you see the lesson in this story as it relates to your role as a manager and leader? The doctor (the general) has the power to reverse ill feelings with a simple attention-giving drop-in between appointments. Unbelievable.

So as you go about your day to day, please keep the point of this writing in mind. As the general, you have the ability to build relationships with new prospects and to create deeper connections with existing clients. It's up to you to be on the lookout for opportunities to make deposits through touch-points and check-ins, and maybe even a lightning-fast, between-appointment, thank-you handshake.

CHAPTER 6

FOCUS ON YOUR CAREER

The biggest rival I had in my career was me.
- Jack Nicklaus

ALL YOU NEED IS TWENTY SECONDS OF INSANE COURAGE

It was time for our weekly family movie night and the kids picked *We Bought A Zoo*. The movie is based on a true story and features Matt Damon as a widowed dad who tries to make a fresh start by buying a broken down zoo. To my surprise, the movie was pretty entertaining, and as a bonus, provided a quote with a real-life application for sales professionals. Matt Damon tries to connect with his onscreen son by offering the following advice: "You know, sometimes all you need is twenty seconds of insane courage. Literally, just twenty seconds of embarrassing bravery. And I promise you, something great will come of it."

Do you remember as an account executive

sitting in the parking lot of a new business prospect? You sat there staring through the windshield, relieved when you spotted the owner serving a client. "They can't talk to me now, they're with a client," you justified to yourself. "Maybe I'll swing by the car dealer and pick up a tape and then come back here to see if the owner is free." Inevitably, when you stopped by the new business later in the day the parking lot was filled with cars. "No way the owner can see me now—too many customers," you happily told yourself before heading back to the office.

Little did you know, the cars in the parking lot belonged to your media competition and at that very moment, in an audience with the new business owner, the competition was stealing your potential commission. You were the victim of a classic case of call reluctance.

Be honest with yourself. Doesn't call reluctance rear its ugly head at every level of your career? As a sales manager, we have all felt the split-second hesitation before calling a key client to work through the wrongs of a rogue AE. As a general manager, you have caught yourself taking a deep breath before addressing the upset, big-spending auto dealer and his complaint over your station's news coverage. Even today, I'm feeling a bit of call reluctance over a few diagnosis phone calls with group heads taking place this afternoon. Are they happy? Do they like the service we're providing?

The root of call reluctance begins with the "what if's?" Nine times out of ten the "what if's" never show their ugly head and we end the visit feeling positive. However, to get to the call we need a breakthrough—something to push us beyond the voice in our head telling us that we "can't." In these instances, all you need is twenty seconds of insane courage. Try it sometime. And I promise you, something great will come of it.

BATTLING THROUGH A SLUMP

Have you ever seen an interview where a professional athlete explains in frustration the reality of career peaks and valleys? For some reason, the planets stop aligning and the athlete temporarily loses their "mojo." In sports terms, the athlete is in a "slump." Typically, the interview with a sports star in a slump ends with the athlete committing to re-dedicate themselves to a few small details that are seemingly responsible for holding back peak performance.

The same scenario applies to media sales managers. Many anticipate and recognize that performance valleys are inevitable. How quickly a manager responds to correcting the slump helps separate a star manager from a mediocre manager.

Throughout my management career, when

battling through a slump, I have found it useful to re-dedicate my personal accountability in five key areas:

1. **Yourself.** Apply yourself and develop your talent to the fullest capacity—without excuses. Are you making an honest daily effort to see as many clients as possible? Are you positioning yourself and your media for the order? Are you the example by always asking for the client investment? Do you encourage local direct business as the foundation of your revenue plans? Keep your focus in check by asking, "Is my effort at this very second making money?"

2. **Your Talent.** Do not waste talent. Put it to great use in the service of something outside of yourself. Doing so can bring immense personal fulfillment and helps to create a positive environment. Watch how your goals are achieved when you apply your talent to help those around you to achieve their goals.

3. **Your Career.** Act "as if" you have been to the peak before. Your actions should reflect the highest standards, especially in the face of opposition. Differentiate to separate and make yourself memorable among the mass of media managers and sellers.

4. **Your Clients**. Show respect to those who come to you with need. Clients are depending on you

to show them the "way" to marketing success. That's a huge responsibility that if handled correctly and professionally will reward you with unsolicited referrals. Never forget that success creates luck.

5. **Your Team**. Act as a mentor to those who sincerely seek your leadership. Share with them the voice of your experience. Remind them that one individual does not make a team. In stressful situations, avoid the verbal negatives. Teach the team that an honest reflection of personal accountability comes before team accountability.

A SOLUTION FOR YOUR LACK OF SLEEP

Before there were smartphones and tablets I used to end the night lying in bed next to the dim glow of a night light reading either a John Grisham legal thriller or a business book. Reading helped calm my thoughts from the day's management issues and always seemed to add weight to my eyelids making going to sleep and staying asleep fairly easy tasks.

Then, through the advent of technology, I was able to leave the books with paper on the shelf and enjoy reading electronically from an iPad. The dim glow of a night light was replaced by the glow of the tablet screen. Likewise, electronic books soon gave way to surfing the Internet for more important worldly information such as background information on *Survivor* contestants or what happened to the 3rd place finisher in season 4 of *American Idol*?

Shortly thereafter, a habit began to form that had a dramatic negative effect on my ability to get a good night's rest. The last thing I did before turning off my iPad and closing my sleepy eyes was check email. My nights of blissful slumber came to a screeching halt. Why? Inevitably, in the final evening emails there would be one or two "sticky" issues that had to be addressed. Maybe the email was an unhappy client or an employee request for help. Regardless, it was these kinds of emails that got the brain excited to pull a "fretting over the issues" all-nighter while the rest of my body was fighting to stop staring at the ceiling from 2 to 5 a.m.!

Is this relatable? If so, and you long for the past nights of restful slumber, I have a solution for you. Don't check email before you go to sleep!

Managing sales teams can be hard mental work. It's the kind of work that can sometimes make it difficult to quiet one's brain. It would make sense then that the last thing you should be doing is thinking about work while you're trying to go to sleep to rest and forget about work! So don't check your email before you go to sleep.

For you naysayers, I have an astounding

surprise. Like you, I was skeptical when I considered the thought of going to sleep without checking email. To my amazement, the very next morning, and every morning thereafter upon waking and taking a quick glance at my smartphone, all of the previous night's emails were sitting right there in the inbox. Wow. This discovery was kind of like when we were kids trying to determine if the light stayed on when we shut the refrigerator door.

If you still aren't convinced, consider this. When was the last time your station engineer emailed you to tell you the station is off the air? Hopefully never. News like that should be handled with an emergency phone call. My point? If it's important enough—absolutely urgent—people will call you and get you out of bed.

The nice thing about waiting until the next morning to check email is that with a quiet brain you'll be more relaxed, well rested, and much better prepared to respond to any issues that may have been sent your way the night before.

ARE YOU COMMITTED?

Mark Sanborn (www.marksanborn.com) is an acclaimed keynote speaker and best-selling author of 8 books on leadership, customer service, and extraordinary performance. One of my favorite books from Mark is *Fred 2.0: New Ideas on How to Keep Delivering Extraordinary Results.* The book is a follow-up to Mark's *Fred Factor*, about a real-life mailman who has turned an ordinary job into something extraordinary. As a result of Mark's books, companies across the country have created programs to develop their own teams of dedicated "Freds."

The word "commitment" was a strong theme throughout *Fred 2.0.* Mark feels that commitment is a decision, not a feeling. It's a promise or pledge you make to others or to yourself. In my early years as an account executive, I was taught to *under promise and over deliver.* In other words, if I was going to commit to someone's expectations, I had better deliver or they would find someone else to take care of their needs.

Our industry has changed dramatically. Sellers juggle budgets for multiple stations, channels, non-traditional, digital, and corporate projects. And you, as a manager, are under pressure every day to make sure all efforts are on course to set new revenue goals. We're always chasing a number. Even the most well-intentioned individuals could inadvertently miss a few deadlines or, worse yet, over promise and under deliver. In this environment, I have observed that some sellers, and even a few managers, are burned out. They have lost their commitment.

So what's the fix? The first step is reminding

yourself that you have a choice. It is your choice to come to work every day deciding to make a positive difference, or you can drag into work making excuses and sinking deeper into a cloud of negativity. Understand that having a bad day on occasion is okay. It happens to everyone. However, winners are able to recover from a bad day and get back on track with their commitment. Mark Sanborn describes 3 characteristics of committed people. They are great examples that managers in our changed industry would be wise to consider.

1. Committed people are generally happy.

Not everything we must do every day makes us happy.

In a Jim Doyle & Associates Leaders Edge tele-seminar, self-discipline strategist and best-selling author Rory Vaden (www.roryvaden.com) stated, "Every single top producer has formed the habit of doing things even when they don't feel like doing them." Mark Sanborn explains that how we choose to do things has a significant impact on the emotions we experience. Doing an unpleasant task cheerfully trumps doing a pleasant task begrudgingly.

2. Committed people are clear about what they do and why they do it.

Here, Mark advises to strive to make the process itself your reward. If you set out to do something for a benefit or payment that doesn't happen, you may feel as though you have wasted your time and you may be disappointed. However, if you set out to do something because you will enjoy doing it regardless of the outcome, then any kind of tangible reward is icing on the cake.

3. Committed people have goals.

Build your commitments around a desire to deliver a positive outcome. What kind of difference do you want to make? Who do you want to influence? In order to get there, you're going to need a map or goals. Write them down, hold yourself accountable, and follow through.

Ultimately, as Mark wrote, when you take the step from being merely involved to being truly committed, everyone benefits—your company, your family, and especially you.

THE ABSOLUTE BEST SALES MANAGER I EVER WORKED FOR WAS THE BEST BECAUSE...

As you have continued your career climb, have you ever wondered or studied what makes a great manager great? Probably the best way to answer this question is to pose the question to those who have worked for a person whom they considered to be their best ever manager. So I posed a question to members of our Jim Doyle & Associates team: "The absolute best sales manager I ever worked for was the best because..." Their interesting answers and advice follow:

From Elaine Lunkes

The absolute best sales manager I ever worked for was always "present" when she met with you. She gave you her complete attention and, as a result, you consistently felt like she truly cared for your success. When you needed help, she stayed on your agenda (unlike another boss I had—every time I went to her to discuss something in my world, she'd change the topic to what I could do to help with hers.) When I was down, she ALWAYS picked me up and convinced me I could do it. She was even tempered, never about placing blame—it was about what we CAN do. When I was up for a promotion outside of her responsibility, she was 100% supportive. I got the job and lost the best boss I ever had.

From Anne Fowler

The absolute best sales manager I ever worked for empowered me to make the tough decisions about my accounts. It was as if I were running my own business. In a pinch, the manager was always available to offer a different perspective or additional insight. As a result, I never felt like I was "going it alone" with my business.

In contrast, one of the worst sales managers I had would "poll" for your best ideas and then turn around and sell them up the pipeline as if they had personally generated the idea!

From Tom Conway

The absolute best sales manager I ever *worked for* was the best because they took the time to know and understand my strengths and consistently put me in a position to best utilize those strengths.

The absolute best sales manager I have ever *observed or worked with* was the best because they had a strategy and a plan that was clearly communicated to their team. Everyone possessed buy-in to the vision. They were on the same page, and as a result, it positively impacted the bottom line.

From Perry Kapiloff

When we were both much younger, Don Fitzgibbons (another JDA Senior Marketing Consultant) was the GM/GSM for a radio station we worked for back in the mid 1980's. The station had a very limited signal and wasn't a big player in Arbitron. It was an AM in a world of FM stations, yet we produced the most local direct revenue in the market. I'm quite sure we performed 3-4 times better than we should have based on the station's situation.

Don convinced us that if we were the only ones working the streets we could take advantage of the "Fat Cats" at the bigger, more listened to stations and make a lot of money. There were always incentives on the table. Because of a limited sales incentive budget, the prizes weren't big payoffs but they were always fun. Every Friday at 4:30pm, we had our "Fat Cat Meeting," where we would throw darts at the poster of big Fat Cats each featuring an easily identified station logo on its chest.

Dart throws were earned through incremental sales that were made that week. The payoff depended upon where the dart landed. Looking back, attendance, while not mandatory, was close to 100% each week. It became a big competition among the sales force on who would get the most darts on Friday. Fun is the operative word here. The atmosphere was fun, the competition was fun, and I know other stations in the market always wanted to know how we out-billed them locally.

My manager let us go do our job and be on the streets making calls—not doing a series of reports telling him how we were occupying our time. The sales meetings each week were short and many included music, a guest speaker or an off-site visit somewhere. It was a laid-back environment, but we consistently won the revenue game.

From David Melville

The absolute best sales manager I ever worked for possessed many great qualities. She had integrity beyond reproach. She was consistent so you always knew where she stood. She was "hands off" and let her sales team members do their thing—as long as they were making budget! She was always there when you needed her and she stood by and supported her people. She always paid attention and provided that perfect balance of oversight and freedom.

From Phil Bernstein

The sales manager who stands out may not have been, on a day-to-day basis, the best manager, but when he had to deliver a piece of bad news, he took some steps that had huge meaning for my career.

He was the VP of Sales and I was (at the time) the LSM of KEX radio. He called me in one day to tell me that I was no longer going to be the sales manager and asked me to go back on the floor as an account executive. I was to receive a pretty substantial open list. He told me he had no confidence in me as a manager, but that I was one of the best salespeople he'd ever seen and he wanted to keep me in the building. I asked him to give me the weekend to think about it.

I came back on Monday with a proposal to sell the entire 5-station cluster, with no account list. I wanted to build my own list from scratch, using nothing but local direct. I had the benefits to the company detailed in the proposal, and wanted a significant monetary guarantee. Among the perks I asked for was a $1,500 per year budget I could use for training. He could have told me to get out of his office, but instead he went upstairs to the market manager, presented it, and fought for it.

Three days later I was the only person on the staff selling the full cluster. I didn't get all the perks I asked for (alas, no covered parking), but I did get the financial guarantee—and the training budget. I spent every dime of that training budget. Among the things I spent it on were some CD's and a subscription to a publication called *Auto Revenue Insights* from some guy named Jim Doyle.

From Pat Norris

Those who were positive, listened, patient, and who "taught not told" were the absolute best sales managers I've ever had. They held me accountable and responsible. They had some rules that were bendable and some that were non-negotiable. They communicated clear expectations, gave consistent feedback about what needed to be changed in my behavior, and were process-oriented. They also asked for honest input and feedback from their team.

From Don Fitzgibbons

This is going to sound like a blatant attempt to score points, but I nominate Jim Doyle as the best ever sales manager from my early radio days, circa 1978. He was the LSM at WLAM AM Radio in Auburn, Maine.

But lest we crown Jim with too much skill and cunning, I should clarify the circumstances and logic behind my nomination:

a) He was the only broadcasting sales manager I ever had. After that, I became the sales manager, then the owner, etc.

b) His outstanding management virtue was that he never managed me. You have to remember that I was an ex-fighter pilot, car salesman, lobster peddler, and stock broker. I was prone to operating in my own egotistical solo world. I made sales calls on my motorcycle, just like Tom Cruise. I knew everything, at least I thought I did, and therefore needed no help from anyone.

So, Jim smartly allowed me the freedom to do what I did best—sell.

The only time we met for any managing type stuff was when I brought in an order. He always gratefully accepted whatever it was. Big or small, no matter the dollar total on the order, it was praised. My natural tendency was to work hard and even more-so, I hated failure. If I had been criticized or chastened for any misdemeanor, it would have crushed my sales spirit.

Thankfully, praise and a generous "thanks for the order" high-five were all I ever got from Jim.

In my opinion, managers would do well today to understand that one size does not fit all. Each of your sellers has a unique and distinct persona.

For many, a hands-off style of managing would fail. But in my case, given my personality, the best management style was a bit of non-management.

SOMETIMES A MIRROR IS THE BEST MANAGEMENT TOOL

Upon returning from a client call trip, I took a little time for reflection. What I really wanted to do was think through my suspicion. You know, one of those, "Is what I'm seeing and hearing really going on?" Unfortunately, the answer seemed to be a resounding "yes."

When television sales professionals benefit from slight regional upticks in a few advertising categories, the sales teams in those markets are happy. However, not surprisingly, the opposite is also true. Locations where those upticks haven't occurred and times are tough and commission checks lower, the sales teams in these markets *are not* happy.

My belief is that energy, whether positive or negative, is transferred from one to another. For some reason, I am a magnet for negative energy. Sales managers and reps in the unhappy markets seem to have a difficult time overcoming their supposed economic adversity and feel compelled to share their negativity with me. They wax poetic about the massive political revenue heydays of past years and, "Why can't today be the same?" Quite honestly, the conversations are difficult for me to get through. Right or wrong, listening to the doom and gloom only reinforces and gives credibility to the concern.

Please don't misunderstand me. When the industry was in a true economic depression I was not some "pie in the sky" optimist who hung an *I refuse to participate in the recession* bumper sticker on my hybrid. But I will not bury my head in the sand and simply "wait out" the tough times. Author and speaker, Price Pritchett, advises one to, "Examine your own attitude. Evaluate your personal investment in pushing for change." He ends with, "Sometimes the best management tool is a mirror." Are you listening to your staff? Is it time to turn the mirror on them?

Ah, the mirror. A great tool for holding yourself accountable for your future. The reflection displays the only person who is capable of helping you get your head out of the sand. *"YOU are the master of every situation,"* explains a Chinese proverb. My suggestion is to empower yourself to be an agent of change. Change opinion among all the naysayers you meet by transferring positive energy. Be there to listen, but leave the conversation on an upswing. Think in terms of building brand equity for your clients through the incredible power of marketing exposure on your outlet. Have you considered introducing multiple buyers or clients to one another to take advantage of the power of testimonials? For example, "I hear your situation and have been there. This is what we did." While everyone else is reinforcing the negative air, you, as a manager and leader, have the opportunity to differentiate by simply offering troubled souls a smile and sincere concern for the betterment of their business and yours. But, there has to be action. Doing "nothing" does not ring the cash register.

It is my belief that the bad times are necessary because without the bad times, how would we ever be able to recognize and enjoy the good times? I'm excited about the future and the opportunities that lie ahead in our business. How about you?

WHAT DO I HAVE TO LOSE?

I was in Tallahassee enjoying lunch with Heather Peeples, one of our partner station General Sales Managers, and their Digital Manager, Ryan Barber. We were in a restaurant with close tables, where most conversations were within earshot. At some point during the lunch I was having a hard time understanding Heather. There was an attorney speaking with his client in the booth behind us and he seemed oblivious to all the other diners as he loudly spewed a bit of attorney-client privileged information.

Lunch continued and so did the attorney. We were actually having difficulty carrying on our own conversation as the lawyer wove one story into the next. Eventually, the stories stopped and the attorney shifted gears into his wisdom on advertising. Our table sat silent, taking in our neighbor's thoughts on the pros and cons of radio, television, and newspaper advertising. We could barely contain our excitement upon hearing, "...that's why I think I am ready to try television advertising."

What would you have done in this situation? What would your AE's do in this situation? I'm guessing there are those who would feel uncomfortable speaking to the attorney, as doing so would be admitting to "listening in" on a private conversation. (Did I mention this guy was loud?)

This GSM's next move is what separates average from great. Heather stated, "After we pay the check, I'm going to introduce myself to the attorney. What do I have to lose, right?"

After lunch, Ryan and I excused ourselves while Heather approached the attorney's booth. Professionally and confidently, while presenting her business card, she began to speak, "Excuse me. I apologize for interrupting your lunch but I could not help but overhear that you are ready to explore the power of television advertising. My name is Heather Peeples. I'm the General Sales Manager of WCTV Television."

The lawyer shook her hand as she continued, "Our station has a reputation for helping local advertisers get powerful results with their hard-earned advertising investment. Would it make sense for us to get together to discuss your needs; to see if we might be able to help with your marketing goals?"

Wow! Heather did *two* things right in this scenario:

1. **She recognized opportunity**
2. **She immediately acted on the moment. In her words, she empowered her "what do I have to lose" attitude**

How much better could you be if you empowered that type of attitude in the split seconds that opportunity passes? Allow me to compound the question—how much better could your team be if you conditioned *all* of your sellers to recognize and act upon these moments?

So the final question is, did Heather's display of confidence work? Yes, so far. Heather emailed me to say she and an AE are scheduling an appointment to see the attorney. Why wouldn't they? What do they have to lose?

Update: As of this 2016 writing, Heather is now Vice President & General Manager (can you see why?) of WCTV in Tallahassee, FL, and

WSWG in Albany, GA. I asked her if the attorney ever ended up advertising with them. "As a matter of fact, yes!" she stated. "I don't know how much my 'interruption' of his lunch influenced his decision but it certainly didn't hurt. I immediately put an AE on this and they found out that a small local agency had just begun working with him. He became an advertiser shortly after that!"

What a great story.

THE THREE PHASES OF CAREER THINKING

I'm approaching the back third of my career. That sounds kind of funny coming from a guy that's only 48 years old. But thankfully, I don't mean the back third in terms of age. No, instead, this back third reference is in terms of thinking.

Remember your post-college job hunt? You were trying to get your foot into any media outlet that cracked their door open to take a look at you. Money wasn't the issue, getting the job was the priority because you knew in this first phase of career thinking that if only you were given the opportunity, you were going to perform and the money would follow.

In the second phase of career thinking, many times we're burning the candle at both ends, trying to outperform peers to get the promotions, titles, money, and the increased responsibility to make decisions to affect change. Typically, this is the period of biggest life maturation as we are working just as hard to raise a family and provide our kids a foundation of success.

In the back third of career thinking, I have discovered that while money is still important, the priorities begin to shuffle a bit. Life now isn't so much about the climb, it's more about the give back—the legacy. The legacy is not a personal one or focusing on how people remember John Hannon, instead, it's how can I be better for those around me now so that ultimately I can have a positive impact on the future of those who will one day be walking these hallways?

Where are you in your career thinking? More importantly, where are your team members in their career thinking? If you don't know, now might be a great time for you, as the leader, to ask. It's likely a question your sellers have rarely if ever heard and it just might be the spark of attention that brings you closer and kindles a mentorship.

DOES YOUR JOB BRING YOU JOY?

Think about the things and moments in life that bring you great joy. They fill you with immense satisfaction and your face widens with a smile. Producing energy, passion, dedication, and commitment for the things and moments you love comes easily.

As you reflected on the joy and love in your life, did your career path come to mind? Right now, look around your office and take in the sight of your (assumedly hard-working) team. Can you honestly say, "I am having an impact; I am happy and I belong here"?

As I travel the country, it's disappointing to hear the number of leaders, managers, and friends in our industry who are unhappy in their jobs. These are the unhappily employed. In my opinion, life is too short and the suffering isn't worth it.

During an interview on one of our Jim Doyle & Associates Leaders Edge tele-seminars with Marshall Goldsmith, renowned leadership thinker and best-selling author, Marshall explained that if you don't love what you do you are living in the "new-age professional hell." He advises that we don't have to love everything we do, but we need to find happiness and meaning in most of our professional work.

Many years ago, people worked 40 hours a week and maxed out their vacations. Further, a one- or sometimes two-week vacation generally provided a full personal battery recharge, as there was no connection to the office. As a result, one could tolerate not thoroughly enjoying their job.

In today's environment, the expectation is a 50, 60, or even 70-hour work week. Vacation lengths are shorter—maybe as short as an extended weekend. Do you ever hear of a two-week personal vacation anymore? In addition, work never really stops thanks to smartphone technology and the constant flow of after work and vacation texts and emails. This always-connected expectation makes for a very stressful and unhappy existence for those who don't enjoy their job.

If you find yourself falling into the category of the unhappily employed, you have *three* options:

Option 1: Don't change a thing. Continue to be filled with anxiety on the drive into the office, especially Monday mornings. As the years pass, you'll become bitter and negative, which will spread through the office like cancer. You will never maximize the potential joy of life because the majority of your waking hours will be spent in dread. You deserve better.

Option 2: You are a manager and a leader. (Only you can determine in what order.) As a result, you have the power to improve your surroundings. Take stock of your operation. What are the barriers preventing you from enjoyment in your role? Lay out a vision, get buy-in from the team, and begin to create an environment fertile with laughter, fun, and reward.

I know what some of you are thinking. "Sometimes my own manager is one of the barriers!" Make sure you have thoroughly reviewed the reflection in the mirror before making that accusation. Is there something you are doing that is reinforcing the negative treatment from your own boss or could your boss be included among the unhappily employed? How must the team feel if the top tier of managers are unhappy in their roles? That's a deeper conversation for another time.

Option 3: The third option is a gut check. Did you make a mistake when you chose a television sales career path? To help you determine your answer I want to share something my uncle once told me, "You're going to have unhappy days at work. But when the number of *unhappy* days exceeds the number of *happy* days, it may be time to question if you're on the right career path."

If your answer dictates that it's time for a career change, that's okay. There's still a lot of life left to determine what you really want to be when you grow up. Hopefully, you'll find something that makes you sincerely happy!

THE FINAL LESSON

I DIDN'T KNOW WHAT I DIDN'T KNOW

It was a week before my 47th birthday and Bridget and our three kids were laughing loudly. We're a family that likes to share and have fun at our evening meal, so laughing wasn't out of the norm. But this time the family was laughing *at* me, not *with* me. Apparently, I had said something funny, and for the life of me, I couldn't get the table to settle down so I could ask them what they found so hilarious.

Finally, through the cackling, Bridget was able to get a question in, "Do you really think that ponies grow into adult horses?"

The table went deadly silent in anticipation of my answer.

"Yes?" I replied hesitantly, trying to save face and act as if I might be teasing in the way-off chance I could be wrong.

Everyone, including I'm convinced our dogs, burst into a shriek.

For nearly 47 years I thought a pony was the

name for a baby horse and, as a result, had always assumed that ponies grew into full blown adult horses. Who knew that ponies and horses weren't one in the same?!

I didn't know what I didn't know.

In our industry, I unfortunately sometimes encounter managers who are close to having their own revelation similar to my pony and horse experience. Except in these instances, no one is laughing.

These managers play everything safe or middle of the road. They don't value sales training or even meetings to organize a sales front, nor do they believe in investing in themselves through books, training or workshops.

Many of these executives are stuck in a fearful "what if" gear and are quick to present a case for why something *can't* or *will not* happen. The word "aggressive" is not in their vocabulary, as it elevates thoughts of offending currently investing clients. Accountability escapes them and they're unable to inspire their sales teams to new performance levels.

The bosses of these types of individuals become frustrated pushing for anything that's higher than flat or low single digit revenue increases. The seller who works for this kind of manager is often wondering when the leader is going to show and if this person is really suited to be their manager.

In the end, when the manager finally does gain clarity and admits, "I didn't know what I didn't know," it's often too late.

Because you've read this book, it's not too late for you. You have made what I hope you consider a wise investment of your time.

Your challenge now is to put into action the information you have gained. This is your opportunity to be the industry example of a model manager and leader. Engage your teams, inspire them to win, and confidently guide them to never-before-seen levels of performance!

ABOUT THE AUTHOR

John Hannon is President of Jim Doyle & Associates, a marketing firm of speakers, authors, trainers, and consultants that in 2015 made over 5,000 sales calls and closed over $50,000,000 in digital and television revenue for their 97 partner stations.

John travels the country as an in-demand industry speaker. He works with television companies to develop profitable strategies for both media outlets and client advertisers. His extensive knowledge of television management, marketing, digital convergence, and sales enables him to help industry leaders create powerful selling cultures to significantly grow their businesses.

His broadcasting career began at the age of fifteen as a radio station disc jockey. By the age of eighteen, John answered the call of customer service as an account executive.

He offers clients an impressive portfolio of experience having held various sales, station management, program distribution, and corporate positions with Tri-Radio Broadcasting, ACT III, Sullivan Broadcasting, Sinclair Broadcasting, Quorum Broadcasting, and Acme Communications. Under John's leadership, television stations have won five #1 in the nation awards, the network Model For Success, the Better Business Bureau Integrity Award, and multiple National Association of Broadcasting Sales Promotion awards.

Originally from Ironton, Ohio, John holds degrees from Central Texas College and Ohio University. He completed his Master's degree in Journalism and Broadcast Station Management at Marshall University. He is a member of the National Speakers Association.

John is a nearly twelve-year veteran of the Air Force, Air Force Reserve, and Army National Guard. He is a retired rugby player living in Sarasota, Florida with wife Bridget, two daughters, a son, and two dogs.

EXPERIENCE
DOYLE ON DEMAND

The Television Industry's Premier Sales Training Platform

A multi-million dollar virtual interactive sales training platform, with 24/7 access via mobile, tablet, computer, or any electronic device that has Internet capability.

For the rookie seeking that first sale to sales veterans looking for new revenue highs, and managers and leaders bent on building the best sales organizations in the industry, Doyle on Demand offers multiple interactive training courses and chapters designed to make you money and make you better.

THE LEADERS EDGE
COACHING PROGRAM

Let's face it. Our business is getting more difficult and complex every day. Change is occurring at the speed of light and it's your job to develop strategies and tactics and, even more importantly, to motivate your team to capitalize on these changes and lead them to success.

But you can't do it alone! You need a leadership coach—more specifically, a PERSONAL leadership coach! THE LEADERS EDGE PROGRAM is just that... a comprehensive personal coaching program specifically designed for TV and Cable sales managers. If *Engaged Management* has made an impact on you, then you'll want to check out this ongoing, multi-formatted, real-world program that's guaranteed to help you become a stronger leader. And great sales organizations are the result of STRONG LEADERSHIP!

CONTACTS

John M. Hannon
Jim Doyle & Associates, Inc.
7711 Holiday Drive
Sarasota, FL 34231

941-926-7355
john@jimdoyle.com
www.jimdoyle.com
www.doyleondemand.com

 /johnhannonmedia

 /in/johnhannonmedia

 /johnhannonmedia

 @johnhannonmedia

 /JimDoyleandAssociates

 /company/jim-doyle-&-associates

 /TVJimDoyle

34051615R00116

Made in the USA
San Bernardino, CA
18 May 2016